Foreword
Descriptiv
Measurin
Keep Your Catch Fresh 5
Deflating A Fish's Swim Bladder . . . 5
Removing a Hook 8
Why We Have to Have Rules 9
Freshwater Species 16
Noxious Species 35
Molluscs 39
Crustaceans 44
Saltwater Species 49
Index 133
Further Reading iii

ISBN 0 646 34431 5

AGDEX: 486/00

First published 1997

Information contained in this publication is provided as general advice only. For application to specific circumstances, seek professional technical advice.

The Department of Primary Industries, Queensland, and the Queensland Fisheries Management Authority have taken all reasonable steps to ensure the information contained in this publication is accurate at the time of publication. Readers should ensure that they make appropriate enquiries to determine whether new information is available on a particular subject.

Text prepared by Kym McKauge, Project Officer, EDFISH, Department of Primary Industries, Queensland.

Original concept, editing, design and published by
The Great Outdoors Publications, PO Box 1688, Coorparoo MDC Qld 4151.
Printed by Harding Colour, 7 Proprietary Street, Tingalpa Qld 4173.

FOREWORD

We are becoming increasingly aware of the importance of our fisheries and habitat resources and how valuable they are, not only as a basis for leisure activities but also as sources of good and satisfying food. We also value our freshwater and coastal areas as pleasant places to live, and so we build in and around our fisheries habitats.

Queensland's fisheries cover a wide range of aquatic habitats, from our western rivers, lagoons and waterholes, our freshwater dams and lakes, to our estuaries, reefs, and coastal and offshore deep waters.

Our fisheries resources — commercial, recreational and traditional — are a significant part of our lives, and heritage for our children. Understanding how our resources "live", and what we must do to look after them to keep them healthy and productive, is important for the continued quality of life that we cherish in Queensland.

This book covers a wide variety of freshwater and marine fish species encountered by anglers and lovers of seafood in Queensland. While notes have been provided covering information on the different species' identification and habitat needs, the book is not intended as an in-depth scientific or management document. Officers of the Queensland Boating and Fisheries Patrol and the Queensland Fisheries Management Authority are able to provide information on current bag limits and other management measures.

The Fish Guide will provide for you an excellent reference to our fisheries resources. I trust you will enjoy this publication.

J Pollock
Executive Director, DPI Fisheries Group

Descriptive Points of a Fish or a Crab

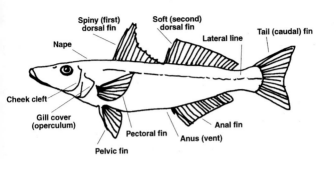

Spiny (first) dorsal fin
Soft (second) dorsal fin
Lateral line
Tail (caudal) fin
Nape
Cheek cleft
Gill cover (operculum)
Pectoral fin
Anus (vent)
Anal fin
Pelvic fin

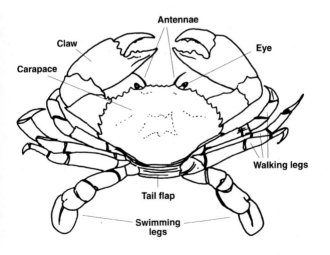

Antennae
Claw
Eye
Carapace
Walking legs
Tail flap
Swimming legs

Measuring Your Catch

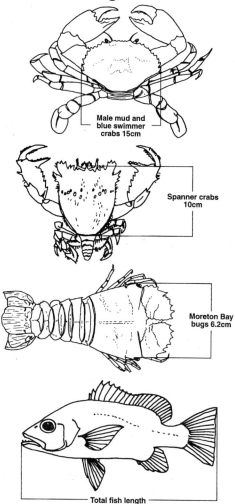

Male mud and blue swimmer crabs 15cm

Spanner crabs 10cm

Moreton Bay bugs 6.2cm

Total fish length

Keeping Your Catch Fresh

All fish should be chilled as soon as possible after being taken from the water.

Crushed or flaked ice is commonly used to chill whole or gutted-and-gilled fish. About 1kg of ice chills 3kg of whole fish for 24 hours. For longer periods, use the same weight of ice as there is of fish.

The quickest way to chill whole fish is by immersing it in a slurry of seawater (or freshwater in the case of freshwater fish) and ice. Freshly caught fish that are properly chilled in ice will have a shelf life of 10 to 12 days. After that time, you have to freeze the fillets to prevent spoilage. Fillets frozen in this way will have little, if any, shelf life remaining and should be cooked immediately after thawing.

Deflating a Fish's Swim Bladder

Many fish use a sac-like organ, called a swim bladder, to maintain neutral buoyancy at various depths in the water. The swim bladder contains gas much like a balloon. The pressure of this gas increases in deep water and decreases in shallow water. Observing fish in a tank demonstrates the value of the swim bladder to fish, as it allows them to maintain a constant depth in the water and conserve their energy to move about. Without the swim bladder, fish "fall" to the bottom.

Sometimes, when fish are pulled quickly to the surface, they cannot adjust the gas in their swim bladders fast enough to cope with the rapid pressure decrease as they are hauled up from the depths. The swim bladder and gut wall may protrude through the mouth (sometimes it may be visible from the vent). If you have caught a fish which you intend to release and its swim bladder is distended, you should carefully attempt to deflate the swim bladder so the fish can return safely to its habitat. Fish may be released without deflating the swim bladder but, as it floats on the surface resorbing excess gas, the risk of predatory attack is high and the fish may not have time to escape.

Fish of the sea perch, snapper and cod families tend to suffer with swim bladder distension.

Do not pierce the swim bladder externally as water may enter the body cavity, leading to the probable death of the fish.

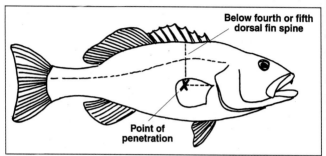

METHOD 1

Using the diagram above as a guide, pierce the area directly below the fourth or fifth dorsal fin spine and immediately behind the upper part of the pectoral fin base.

You should use a clean, sharp instrument which will make only a very small hole, such as a sharp piece of wire, a thin knife point, or a small hollow tube. Successful deflation results in hissing of escaping gas. Immersing the fish in a bucket of clean water will help in determining success (you will see the bubbles of gas). If the hole is small and the instrument clean, the wound should heal quickly.

METHOD 2

A second method of "deflating fish" is currently being tested by fisheries researchers in north Queensland and is practised by commercial reef line fishers.

FISH GUIDE

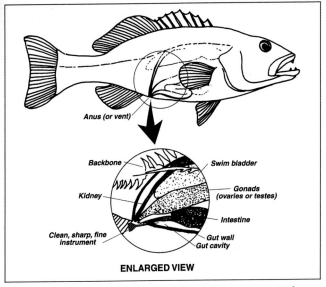

ENLARGED VIEW

This method works on the belief that fish have control over their swim bladder, but not over the gas in their gut cavity. As such, this method involves puncturing the gut cavity to relieve the gas pressure.

It is preferable that a hollow, sterile, metal instrument be used, but success may be achieved with the point of a hook (taking care not to insert the hook past the barb). The affected fish should be held belly-up and the sharp instrument gently inserted into the anterior (towards the head) edge of the anus (or vent) — *See diagram above*. Success is achieved when escaping gas is heard, or seen if the fish has been immersed in clean water.

Gently squeezing the belly will force gas to escape past the end of the hook, or through the hole in the needle. This method requires that the needle or hook is left in while gently squeezing the belly. Otherwise, the hole simply closes up.

Removing a Hook From a Fish

Some guidelines apply to the release of fish (because it is not within legal size or quota (bag) limits, or because you simply may not want to keep it).

HANDLING

When the fish is taken from the water, support its weight and rest it on a wet towel or bag. Try to stop the fish from moving as much as possible by holding and covering its head with a wet towel or your wet hand, taking care not to cause bruising or to remove any scales.

REMOVING TACKLE

Assess whether the hook or lure will be easily removed from the fish's mouth. If so, carefully remove the hook and return the fish gently to the water. Gently "swimming" the fish by holding on to its bottom jaw and leading the fish forward through the water will usually lead to a quick recovery, and the fish should kick free from your grasp.

Should the hook be firmly embedded or swallowed, attempts to remove the tackle will probably result in fatal injury to the fish. In these circumstances, cut off the line as close to the eye of the hook as possible. In many cases, the hook will rust, work its way out of the flesh or be "spat up" (regurgitated) by the fish.

BARRAMUNDI CLOSED SEASON

A CLOSED season applies to barramundi in the Gulf of Carpentaria and adjoining waterways south of the intersection of longitude 142°09' east with the shore at high water mark. This time varies from year to year, depending on the spawning season. Elsewhere, a closure applies from midday, November 1, to midday, February 1, each year. This closure does not apply to fish taken from the area surrounding Tinaroo Dam in north Queensland. However, special provisions apply to barramundi taken from this area during the closed season, such as tagging requirements. Refer to the nearest Queensland Boating and Fisheries Patrol office or the Queensland Fisheries Management Authority for details.

Why Do We Have To Have Rules?

Fish are a finite resource. Their habitats are essential to their future. We cannot take for granted that our fish will always be there. Some species have been lost to us already. Others are bordering on extinction.

Some countries throughout the world have already over-exploited their fisheries resources — they have literally fished out their waters, or destroyed their fish habitats, or both. They didn't recognise the warning signs. They didn't implement and enforce the rules necessary to ensure a future for their natural fisheries. Their authorities didn't alert or educate their people to the need for such protective measures.

Australia can learn from their mistakes. We still have the opportunity to correct our errors of the past and provide for the future — by adopting rules which might in only a few instances limit our fishing in the short term but guarantee our enjoyment of both the recreational and commercial benefits of healthy fisheries resources in the long term.

SIZE LIMITS

Applying size limits to particular species that are harvested is a common practice by resource managers. In Queensland, many fish have minimum legal size limits and some also have maximum legal size limits.

Size limits are based on biological research into each species' reproductive cycles. Minimum size limits allow fish to spawn at least once and to contribute to the growth of that species' population before capture. Some species contribute to the spawning cycle more as they become larger, hence the application of maximum size limits. For example, most barramundi begin their lives as males and later become females, hence the maximum size limit of 120cm applies to protect large females so that they are able to spawn.

BAG LIMITS or QUOTAS

Bag limits (quotas) serve several purposes: to conserve heavily exploited species; to spread the catch more equitably among anglers; and to reduce the illegal marketing of fish.

Quotas are important in highlighting the need for restraint and adoption of a conservation attitude when fishing. Quotas also demonstrate the need for fish which are under heavy fishing pressure to be protected for future sustainability of stocks of that species.

CLOSED SEASONS

Some species, such as barramundi and spanner crabs, are subject to closed seasons. Closed seasons protect fish (or crabs) when they are more vulnerable to fishing pressure. For example, the barramundi closed season is at the time of the year when spawning is taking place.

CLOSED WATERS

Areas closed to fishing protect fish in a variety of ways: where a population of endangered or threatened species lives; where fish congregate at or before spawning; where fish contribute to adjacent areas that are fished; or where fish may mass or be stranded at or near artificial barriers.

GEAR RESTRICTIONS

A variety of restrictions on fishing gear is in force in Queensland. The Queensland Fisheries Management Authority and Department of Primary Industries issue free publications detailing current fishing guidelines. Contact the Queensland Fisheries Management Authority or Queensland Boating and Fisheries Patrol for current information on fishing restrictions and regulations, or ask at your local tackle shop.

WHO MAKES THE RULES?

Fisheries and fish habitats occupy, and are part of, inland, estuarine, coastal and marine ecological systems.

Fisheries are of economic, social, ecological and traditional importance to all Queenslanders. These resources are of special significance to those with interests in commercial fishing, aquaculture, recreation and tourism, and to traditional users — which is just about all of us.

Fisheries resources are available to all of us, and responsibility for their management and good stewardship is a public service shared by government, the resource users and the general public (us).

The Department of Primary Industries, Queensland, and specifically its Fisheries Group, has been charged with providing this management in the areas of: assessing fisheries resources; fish stocking and other forms of enhancement; aquaculture development; protecting habitats; community education; enforcing compliance with rules for sustainable and fair use; boating safety; and shark control.

In this regard, the Fisheries Group conducts research; education and education programs; develops policy and legislation; assists in the development and adoption of new technology; promotes sustainable, profitable and competitive fisheries; monitors the conditions and trends within habitats and stocks; manages fish habitats; promotes community use of fisheries resources; and enforces fisheries laws.

The Group also has overall responsibility for aquaculture industry management, planning, research, education and extension, and fish health services.

The Fisheries Group's partner in fisheries management, the Queensland Fisheries Management Authority (QFMA), develops and implements policies and plans for management of Queensland's various fisheries. This work is largely based on public meetings and discussion papers. The rules which are subsequently formulated are, in effect, what the majority of us have decided we want.

Priority has been given to commercial fisheries productivity, recreational fisheries development, development of the aquaculture industry, protection and management of marine and freshwater fisheries habitats, and the Queensland Boating and Fisheries Patrol services.

The rules are there simply to ensure that all of us can enjoy our fishing interests, whatever they might be, long into the future. And to ensure our children, and their children after them, will also be able to share in those benefits.

DPI FISHERIES

Protecting Our Fishing Future

Coastal wetlands are the areas bounded on the seaward side by seagrass meadows and on the landward side by saltmarshes and ti-tree swamps with mangrove communities in between. Sandbanks and mudflats are also part of our coastal wetlands. Together, these areas constitute an ecosystem which supports our marine fisheries.

A healthy fishing industry relies on the conservation of coastal wetlands as habitat for fish, prawns, crabs and scallops. Wetland areas are important to the lifecycles of estuarine fish species and to the productivity of offshore fisheries which are linked to inshore habitat.

Fish Habitat Areas (tidal and freshwater) form an important component of the protection and management of fisheries resources and wetland habitats in Queensland. These areas are declared with the specific intent of ensuring the continuation of productive recreational, commercial and traditional fisheries in a region.

A Fish Habitat Area may be declared in both marine and freshwater environments to protect important juvenile and adult fish habitats. These habitats include sand bars, shallow water areas, undercut banks, snags, rocky outcrops, pools, riffles, seagrass beds, mangrove stands, yabby banks, etc.

FHAs are declared and managed under the Fisheries Act 1994 and the Fisheries Regulation 1995 by the Department of Primary Industries. Management provides for community use and enjoyment of the area, such as commercial, recreational and traditional fishing and boating, while restricting activities which may have negative impacts on the fisheries and habitat values of the area, such as dredging, reclamation, discharging, drainage, etc.

MARINE PLANTS

All mangroves and other marine plants within Queensland, regardless of growth or the tenure of the lands, are specifically protected by the Fisheries Act.

The term "marine plant" under the Fisheries Act 1994, not only includes those plants normally referred to as mangroves but also includes any other plant that grows on tidal lands, or grows on land adjacent to tidal lands. It includes the material of such plants whether living, dead, standing or fallen. This definition also includes seagrass, saltcouch, samphire vegetation species and other plants growing on tidal lands.

FRESHWATER

Queensland has a greater number of river systems than any other Australian state. Run-off from Queensland's rivers accounts for more than 45% of the total discharge from all Australian rivers. Providing a great diversity of in-stream and associated wetland habitat, Queensland rivers support the most diverse freshwater fish fauna in Australia with about 125 known species of freshwater fish.

Natural rivers and their associated wetlands provide a complex of habitats for a wide variety of animals and plants. The numbers and types of fish species found in a stretch of river is largely dependent on the growth and diversity of suitable habitats available.

In Queensland, human activity has seriously depleted freshwater habitats in some areas, particularly in the south-east of the State. A better understanding and appreciation of these habitats are required if the remaining ones are to be protected for future generations.

DPI FISHERIES

Queensland Boating and Fisheries Patrol

The Queensland Boating and Fisheries Patrol (QBFP) delivers boating safety and fisheries enforcement, surveillance and advisory services throughout Queensland.

The Patrol also manages the Queensland Government Shark Control Program to provide bather protection to many surfing beaches between the Gold Coast and Cairns.

Staff are located at 21 coastal and inland centres to ensure the sustainable use of our fisheries resources and the promotion of safer boating activities.

Community education is considered crucial to achieving these goals. The Patrol has recently introduced the Fishcare Volunteer scheme to enable community-minded citizens to promote the need for sustainable fishing practices and habitat protection. Additionally, displays and other presentations in schools, boat shows, fishing competitions, and the media continue to be utilised to improve community awareness.

Interested persons can also play a major role in protecting resources by reporting any suspected illegal fishing activities on the 24-hour toll-free **Fishwatch Hotline 1800 017 116**, and reporting "off-station" shark equipment or marine animals trapped in shark equipment, by calling the 24-hour toll-free **Shark Hotline 1800 806 891**.

Queensland Fishcare Volunteer Scheme

This project seeks to raise community awareness of and support for the rules and regulations relating to recreational fishing and to improve communication between recreational anglers and fisheries managers.

It also aims to provide an education service to the general angling community regarding fisheries regulations; reduce the take of juvenile and excessive quantities of fish by individuals; disseminate information regarding fisheries regulations; and provide extra monitoring of habitat and advice of changes.

Fishcare Volunteers provide information about rules and regulations relating to recreational fishing; provide advice to recreational anglers about effective angling methods; advise recreational anglers about the release of unwanted and undersized fish; gather data in relation to recreational fishing; monitor habitat and advise of changes; operate only as an extension officer; do not operate as an enforcement officer; do not have any regulatory powers; and do not issue cautions relating to breaches of the regulations.

Contact (07) 3224 2291 for further information.

NATIONAL FISHCARE PROGRAM

An Australia-wide effort to conserve and develop our fish stocks is being co-ordinated by the National Fishcare Program.

The National Fishcare Program for 1996/97 approved grants for 11 projects in Queensland, ranging from ecological and biological studies of the Boondall Wetlands reserve to monitoring the effectiveness of concrete pipes as an inducement to the growth of fish populations on the Curtin Artificial Reef.

The National Fishcare Program is designed to facilitate co-operation and collaboration between the general community, government, industry and scientific institutions. For more information, contact the State Fisheries Action Plan Co-ordinator, Mr Patrick Appleton, on 07 3221 5839.

GUNTHER E. SCHMIDA

Minimum Size: Nil.

Bag Limit: Nil.

Archer fish
(Rifle fish, Spotted bream)

Toxotes **spp.**

DESCRIPTION:

Small to moderate-sized fish growing to 40cm (0.7kg, but more common to 20cm), archer fish have a deep, compressed body, triangular in shape. The top of the fish from the snout to the dorsal fin is almost straight, typical of surface-dwelling fish. They have large eyes and an upward-pointing mouth. Archer fish have bright silvery-green bodies with a number of black blotches along the upper flanks. Three of these blotches are much larger than the others.

HABITAT:

Common in estuaries and freshwaters of northern coastal Australia.

NOTES:

Archer fish are unique in their ability to shoot jets of water accurately more than one metre, to knock insects into the water from overhanging vegetation.

GUNTHER E. SCHMIDA

Minimum Size: 30cm.   **Bag Limit: 2.**

Australian bass

Macquaria novemaculeata

DESCRIPTION:
A large, active fish growing to more than 57cm (3.5kg) but most commonly caught at 1kg. Colouration is dark grey or olive-green along the back, becoming creamy or silvery on the belly. Fish smaller than about 12cm have a large dark blotch on the top of the gill cover.

HABITAT:
In rivers and estuaries in south-east Queensland from Fraser Island and Mary River to the New South Wales border. Natural riverine populations are reduced in numbers and distribution, probably due to habitat loss and construction of dams and weirs which prohibit movement between estuaries and freshwater reaches. Hatchery-reared fingerlings are stocked in many impoundments in south-east Queensland, and provide excellent recreational fisheries.

FISH GUIDE   17

GUNTHER E. SCHMIDA

Minimum Size: 58cm. Max.: 120cm.   **Bag Limit: 5.**

Barramundi
(Giant perch)

Marketing name: Barramundi

Lates calcarifer

DESCRIPTION:

Barramundi are large predators able to adapt to fresh or salt water. They are greenish-bronze along the back, shading to silver along the sides, with white bellies. Young fish often have yellowish pelvic and tail fins. Juveniles have creamy and dark blotches on their bodies.

HABITAT:

Barramundi are found in freshwater lagoons, tidal rivers and estuaries from Maryborough north. Adult fish spawn in coastal seas and estuaries.

NOTES:

Barramundi do not develop their characteristic hump on the nape until adulthood. Juveniles can grow in freshwater environments to a large size, such as the 20cm specimen photographed above, before developing the typical barramundi appearance. Most barramundi begin their lives as males and change to females as they become much larger, hence the maximum legal size limit to protect mature females.

GUNTHER E. SCHMIDA

Minimum Size: Nil.   **Bag Limit: Nil.**

Sooty grunter
(Black bream)

Hephaestus fuliginosus

DESCRIPTION:
A stocky fish known to grow to 50cm (4kg) but more commonly caught at 25cm (0.4kg). Colouration varies from dark brown to sooty black (hence the name), to various shades of brown or gold. Some fish have irregular patches of gold on a dark body.

HABITAT:
The sooty grunter's natural range is in northern Queensland freshwaters throughout the Gulf of Carpentaria and in north-east coastal systems. They prefer rivers with clear flowing water and a sandy or rocky substrate, but have a wide range of environmental tolerance. Some stocking of sooty grunter has been carried out in dams.

NOTES:
Sooty grunter are good eating fish below two kilograms. Fish larger than two kilograms are not considered good eating and should be released.

GUNTHER E. SCHMIDA

Minimum Size: Nil.   **Bag Limit: Nil.**

Bullrout
(Freshwater stonefish)

Notesthes robusta

DESCRIPTION:
Bullrout are a stout, strongly mottled fish. Colours change according to their background, affording them excellent camouflage. Fish grow to 35cm, but are more common at 15cm to 20cm.

HABITAT:
Bullrout are found in estuaries, rivers, streams and creeks along the Queensland east coast, usually in slower-flowing waters among weeds and stones. They are largely inactive, preferring to blend in with the bottom ready to ambush unsuspecting prey, and are difficult to see.

NOTES:
Handle with extreme care. Bullrout have dorsal, anal and pelvic spines armed with venom glands, which may inflict painful injuries.

GUNTHER E. SCHMIDA

Minimum Size: Nil.   **Bag Limit: Nil.**

Eel-tailed catfish
(Freshwater catfish, Dewfish, Tandan)

Marketing name: Freshwater catfish

Tandanus tandanus

DESCRIPTION:
Although reaching sizes of up to 90cm (7kg), most fish are caught below 2.0kg. Eel-tailed catfish are distinctive in having an eel-like tail, scaleless skin and touch-sensitive "whiskers" around their fleshy mouth. Their colour varies. Fish less than 30cm are usually mottled grey. Larger fish may be grey, brown, reddish brown, or olive green with a whitish belly.

HABITAT:
Eel-tailed catfish are found in eastern coastal streams along the Queensland east coast, from the New South Wales border to north of Cairns, and throughout the Darling River. Although still common in Queensland, their numbers are severely reduced in New South Wales and Victoria, causing concern about their conservation status.

NOTES:
Eel-tailed catfish have sharp, strong spines in the dorsal and pectoral fins, which may inflict painful injuries.

GUNTHER E. SCHMIDA

Minimum Size: Nil.

Bag Limit: Nil.

Fork-tailed catfish
(Blue catfish, Salmon catfish)

Marketing name: Blue catfish (*Arius graeffei*)

Arius spp.

DESCRIPTION:

Several species of fork-tailed catfish may be found throughout Queensland. Depending on the species, fork-tailed catfish may grow to 130cm (over 10kg). All display similar characteristics, including a flattened head with barbels ("whiskers") around the mouth, forked caudal fin (tail) and scaleless body. Colouration ranges from black, dark brown, or dark grey to dusky blue, reddish or brownish with golden or bronze patches.

HABITAT:

Fork-tailed catfish are distributed throughout most coastal river systems in Queensland, from upper reaches of rivers, to estuaries and marine environments.

NOTES:

Male fork-tailed catfish incubate their eggs in their mouths (mouth-brooding). Dorsal (back) and pectoral fins have large spines. These fish should be handled with care as they can inflict painful injuries.

GUNTHER E. SCHMIDA

ENDANGERED SPECIES
Mary River Cod
Maccullochella peelii mariensis

DESCRIPTION:
Most Mary River cod are caught at 5kg, but can grow to more than 20kg. They are large, elongated fish with large mouths, slightly concave heads and protruding lower jaws. Colouration is mottled, ranging from golden-yellow to green and dark brown with black to dark green spots.

HABITAT:
Now found naturally in only a few tributaries of the Mary River system. Numbers are known to be very low. Habitat loss is thought to be the major factor in its decline. Stocked specimens may be caught in some south-east Queensland impoundments.

NOTES:
The Mary River cod is listed as a critically endangered species.
Fish may not be taken unless they are caught from listed artificial impoundments (see current Recreational Fishing in Queensland regulations brochure). Currently, a person may take or possess one Mary River cod from waters upstream of Bill Gunn, Cressbrook, Hinze, Maroon, Moogerah, North Pine, Somerset and Wivenhoe Dams.

GUNTHER E. SCHMIDA

Minimum Size: 50cm.

Bag Limit: 5.

Murray cod

Marketing name: Murray cod

Maccullochella peelii peelii

DESCRIPTION:

Murray cod are reported to grow to 180cm (113kg) and are the largest of the Australian native freshwater fishes. Fish are more commonly caught at 55cm to 65cm (2kg to 5kg). Murray cod are mottled in appearance, ranging from brown or olive-green to yellow-green with brown or pale green mottling graduating down to a creamy white belly.

HABITAT:

The natural distribution of Murray cod is the Murray-Darling river systems, west of the Great Dividing Range. They are found in slow-flowing, turbid water where in-stream snags, logs and stumps provide protection and spawning sites.

NOTES:

Murray cod and Mary River cod are closely related and are very similar in appearance. Care must be taken not to confuse the two fish.

GUNTHER E. SCHMIDA

Minimum Size: Nil. **Bag Limit: Nil.**

Sleepy cod
(Sleeper)

Oxyeleotris lineolatus

DESCRIPTION:
Growing to 48cm (3kg), sleepy cod are the largest of the Australian freshwater gudgeons. Sleepy cod are usually caught at an average size of 30cm. Colouration is dark to light brown with spotted fins. The head is flattened and the body elongated.

HABITAT:
Sleepy cod are widespread in central and northern Queensland, from the Dawson River north, and throughout the Gulf of Carpentaria. They are usually found lazing among weedy and quiet areas.

NOTES:
Sleepy cod are excellent eating fish.

Only one hook per line is permitted in freshwater fishing.

GUNTHER E. SCHMIDA

Minimum Size: 30cm.

Bag Limit: Nil.

Freshwater eel

Marketing name: Longfin eel, Shortfin eel, South Pacific eel

Anguilla reinhardtii (Longfin eel)
Anguilla australis (Shortfin eel)
Anguilla obscura (South Pacific eel)

DESCRIPTION:

Reported to reach lengths of more than 200cm, girths of more than 50cm, and weights of more than 20kg, most eels are caught at 100cm. Eels become energetic and difficult to handle when landed. Colouration is olive-green, heavily mottled with darker green, brown and black (longfin eel) or without mottling (adult shortfin eels), or uniformly dark brown (South Pacific eel).

HABITAT:

Eels caught in Queensland are more likely to be longfin eels, as shortfin eels are restricted to more southerly drainages on the Australian mainland. Longfin eels range extensively throughout Queensland in freshwater rivers, dams, lagoons and lakes.

NOTES:

A worthwhile food fish gaining popularity in the marketplace.

GUNTHER E. SCHMIDA

PROTECTED SPECIES **RELEASE UNHARMED**

Queensland lungfish
(Ceratodus)

Neoceratodus forsteri

DESCRIPTION:
Lungfish are large, eel-like fish growing to more than 150cm (40kg). The body is heavy, elongated and covered by large, bony, overlapping scales. The pectoral and pelvic fins are leaf-shaped and resemble flippers. Colouration ranges from dull brown to olive green, with black blotches present on most specimens on the back and sides towards the tail.

HABITAT:
Lungfish inhabit slowly flowing waters. They occur naturally in the Burnett and Mary Rivers but have been introduced to other areas such as the Brisbane River.

NOTES:
Survivors of a group of fishes from some 200 million years ago, the Queensland Lungfish is an ancient and unique species. Although lungfish have well-developed gills, they are capable of gulping air into a lung-like sac, enabling them to survive for extended periods out of the water, or in less-than-favourable water conditions.
Lungfish are totally protected. Special collecting permits, issued under current Fisheries legislation,are issued for specific purposes only (such as scientific research).

GUNTHER E. SCHMIDA

Minimum Size: Nil.

Bag Limit: Nil.

Mouth Almighty

Glossamia aprion aprion
Glossamia aprion gillii

DESCRIPTION:

Mouth almighty are mouth-brooders (they incubate their eggs in their mouths) with large mouths, as the name suggests. They have deep bodies with pointed snouts, with blotchy, dark brown patches over creamy-brown. This colouration gives the mouth almighty excellent camouflage for ambushing prey. Mouth almighty can grow to 20cm (0.6kg) but are more commonly caught much smaller.

HABITAT:

The northern subspecies of mouth almighty (*Glossamia aprion aprion*) are widely distributed north of Mackay, preferring still, weedy, warm freshwaters. The southern subspecies (*Glossamia aprion gillii*) occurs in coastal rivers from the Fitzroy south to the New South Wales border. It has similar habitat requirements.

NOTES:

Male fish incubate the eggs in their mouths. They will stop feeding until the eggs hatch.

GUNTHER E. SCHMIDA

Minimum Size: Nil.   **Bag Limit: Nil.**

Freshwater mullet
(Pinkeye)

Myxus petardi

DESCRIPTION:

Freshwater mullet may grow to 81cm (7.5kg) but are most common at 30cm to 40cm. Sometimes found in schools with sea mullet (which often travel upstream into freshwater), freshwater mullet are easily recognised by their bright orange-yellow eye and dark colouration on their backs.

HABITAT:

Freshwater mullet occur in freshwater reaches of coastal waterways in southern Queensland, travelling to estuaries to spawn in January to March each year.

NOTES:

Although freshwater mullet usually breed in low salinity areas of estuaries, it is believed they are one of the few species able to breed in freshwater impoundments.

GUNTHER E. SCHMIDA

Minimum Size: 30cm.   **Bag Limit: 10.**

Golden perch
(Yellowbelly)

Marketing name: Golden perch

Macquaria ambigua, Macquaria ambigua oriens, Macquaria sp.

DESCRIPTION:

Golden perch are large fish growing to 76cm (23kg) but are more commonly caught around 5kg. Colouration along the back of these fish ranges from dark brown to olive green or bronze, becoming yellow or white towards the belly. Larger adult fish develop a distinctive, humped back.

HABITAT:

Queensland has three genetically distinct stocks of golden perch. One is native to the Lake Eyre drainage system (*Macquaria* sp.), another to the Murray-Darling system (*Macquaria ambigua*) and the last to the Dawson system (*Macquaria ambigua oriens*). The Murray-Darling stock has been introduced into south-east Queensland dams. Golden perch prefer turbid, warmer, slow-flowing streams.

NOTES:

Golden perch are one of the most popular fish stocked in artificial impoundments in Queensland and provide excellent eating.

GUNTHER E. SCHMIDA

Minimum Size: 30cm.   **Bag Limit: 10.**

Silver perch
(Black bream, Bidyan)

Marketing name: Silver perch

Bidyanus bidyanus

DESCRIPTION:
While silver perch are known to grow to more than 7kg, they are more commonly caught between 35cm and 40cm (0.75kg to 1.5kg). Colouration varies from black through to grey, olive green or gold along the back, graduating to grey, greenish, gold, silvery sides, to white belly. The small scales are usually coloured with a dark edge, giving the fish a netted appearance.

HABITAT:
Silver perch occur naturally in the Murray-Darling river system but hatchery-reared fingerlings have been stocked in south-east Queensland impoundments. Natural riverine populations are greatly reduced in numbers throughout the Murray-Darling system and are considered threatened.

NOTES:
Silver perch may be confused with Welch's grunter (*Bidyanus welchi*) which is native to the Lake Eyre drainage.

Minimum Size: Nil.   **Bag Limit: Nil.**

Spangled perch
(Spangled grunter)

Leiopotherapon unicolor

DESCRIPTION:

Spangled perch are small, commonly growing to only 15cm (0.2kg) and rarely grow to more than 25cm (0.6kg). Colouration ranges from brown to grey-blue graduating to a white belly. Mottled, rusty brown spots almost always cover the base colour.

HABITAT:

Spangled perch are distributed naturally throughout Queensland, inhabiting still or slowly flowing waterways, bore drains, billabongs, pools, dams, and all types of natural streams.

NOTES:

Spangled perch are one of the few fish that are able to breed in small dams, having a wide range of environmental tolerances.

GUNTHER E. SCHMIDA

Minimum Size: 35cm.   **Bag Limit: 1.**

Northern saratoga
(Northern spotted barramundi, Gulf saratoga)

Scleropages jardinii

DESCRIPTION:
Very similar to the southern saratoga, the northern saratoga can be differentiated in having three to four orange spots on each scale, which form a crescent pattern. Colouration is dark brown along the back, graduating to a bronze belly.

HABITAT:
Northern saratoga are widely distributed in northern Queensland river systems, south from the Jardine River and throughout the Gulf of Carpentaria. Unlike southern saratoga, the northern species prefers clear streams and rivers, occupying the upper reaches of both fast-flowing streams and still billabongs.

NOTES:
Northern saratoga are one of two Australian surviving ancient species known as the bony-tongue fishes. Saratoga incubate their young in their mouths. Saratoga are excellent sportfish but are not good eating.

GUNTHER E. SCHMIDA

Minimum Size: 35cm.   **Bag Limit: 1.**

Southern saratoga
(Spotted barramundi, Dawson River salmon)

Scleropages leichardti

DESCRIPTION:

Southern saratoga are reported to grow to 90cm (4kg) but are more commonly caught at 50cm to 60cm. Being a surface-dwelling fish, saratoga have an almost perfectly flat back with a dorsal fin set back towards the tail of their long, sleek bodies. Colouration is dark brown to olive green along the back, with lighter sides and a white belly. Small orange or red dots spot most of the large, bony scales.

HABITAT:

The southern saratoga's natural distribution is limited to the Fitzroy River system in central Queensland, but stocks have been established in the Mary, Dawson, Burnett and Burdekin Rivers in southern Queensland. Some dams and rivers in south-east Queensland now also have stocks. Southern saratoga prefer still waters and slow flowing sections of rivers, and are very aggressive and territorial.

NOTES:

Saratoga are surviving members of a group of ancient fishes, dating back between 38 and 55 million years, which have bony tongues. Female saratoga incubate their eggs in their mouths. Saratoga are excellent sportfish but are not good eating.

CRUCIAN CARP — DPI FISHERIES

NOXIOUS FISH

The introduction of exotic fish species into Queensland's natural waterways often leads to a reduction in native fish numbers, or the total exclusion of native species. Exotic fish species affect native species through direct competition for food and space, predation, habitat alteration, and the introduction of exotic diseases and parasites.

Legislation exists under the Fisheries Act (1994) for the management of noxious and non-indigenous fishes in Queensland waters.

Noxious fish are listed in the Regulations of the Fisheries Act. Those species declared noxious in Queensland Waters are:
Carp (*Cyprinus carpio*), piranhas (all species of the family Serrasalmidae), tilapia (all species of the genera *Tilapia, Oreochromis* and *Sarotherodon*), walking catfish (all species of the family Claridae), bluegill (*Lepomis* spp.), electric eel (all species of the family Gymnotidae), grass carp (*Ctenopharyngodon idella*), largemouth bass (*Micropterus salmoides*), mosquitofish (*Gambusia* spp.), Nile perch (*Lates niloticus* — live only), parasitic catfish (all species of the families Trichomycteridae and Vandellinae), pike cichlid

KOI CARP — DPI FISHERIES

(*Crenicichla* spp.), snakehead (*Channa* spp.), tiger shovelnose catfish (*Pseudoplatystoma fasciatum*), tigerfish (Hydrocyninae and Erythrinidae), and Chinese weatherfish (weatherloach) (*Misgurnus anguillicaudatus*).

Fines in excess of $75,000 can be imposed on anyone having noxious fish in their possession without a permit. Noxious fish cannot be kept, hatched, reared or sold. All noxious fish when caught should be destroyed and must not be returned to the water. They must not be used as bait. Persons guilty of releasing noxious fish may be charged with the costs of eradication and removal of those fish.

The Fisheries Regulations list a number of prescribed non-indigenous fish. Prescribed non-indigenous fish may be held in aquaria, above-ground ponds or other enclosures that prevent their escape, but cannot be released into the wild. Examples include the Goldfish (*Carassius auratus*), Rosy Barb (*Puntius conchonius*) and the Guppy (*Poecilia reticulata*).

Persons convicted of releasing species such as the Goldfish (*Carassius auratus*) may incur a penalty of more than $75,000. Additional penalties may be imposed to cover the cost of eradication measures.

DPI FISHERIES

NOXIOUS FISH   **DESTROY**

Carp

(Common carp, European carp, Mirror carp, Koi carp)

Marketing name: European carp

Cyprinus carpio

DESCRIPTION:
Mirror and koi carp are ornamental variations of the wild or common European carp. European carp can grow to more than 120cm (60kg). In Australia, it is more commonly caught at 3kg. Colouration may vary, but it can be distinguished as having a goldfish-like appearance and a pair of barbels ("whiskers") at the corners of the mouth.

HABITAT:
The European carp was imported into Australia as a sportfish and has had a serious destructive effect on Queensland's freshwater environment. Carp are found in the Murray-Darling river system, the Mooloolah and Logan Rivers, and in various dams.

NOTES:
Carp can tolerate extreme environmental conditions, including high turbidity, a wide range of water temperatures, high salinity, and low dissolved oxygen levels. Carp will often survive when water quality is too low to support other fish species.

NOXIOUS FISH   **DESTROY**

Tilapia
(Mozambique mouth brooder)

Oreochromis mossambicus

DESCRIPTION:

This species of tilapia can grow to more than 36cm although stunting may occur when conditions are less than ideal (overcrowding, poor water quality, etcetera). Noxious fish grouped under the name of tilapia also include all species of the genera *Tilapia*, *Oreochromis*, and *Sarotheradon*.

HABITAT:

Tilapia are native to Africa and are now widely distributed and problematic in Queensland. Breeding populations have established in both northern and southern Queensland.

NOTES:

Tilapia are readily able to become the dominant fish species in freshwater and upper estuaries to the detriment of native fish. They successfully invade these areas due to simple food requirements, flexible habitat preferences, wide environmental tolerances, and highly effective reproduction strategies.

FISH GUIDE

MOLLUSCS

A bag limit of 50 molluscs (gastropod or bivalve shells) taken or had in possession at any one time applies to all species except oysters and those specifically protected. Some shells are totally protected and include helmet (*Cassis cornuta*), trumpet or giant triton (*Charonia tritonis*) and clam (family *Tridacnidae*) shells.

Deception Bay, Nudgee Beach and Wynnum, near Brisbane, are closed to the taking of all molluscs. Contact the nearest Queensland Boating and Fisheries Patrol for details and specific closed areas in these places.

DPI FISHERIES

Minimum Size: 9cm (8am, November 1 to 8am, May1)
9.5cm (8am, May 1 to 8am, November 1)

Ballot's saucer scallop

Marketing name: Saucer scallop

Amusium japonicum balloti

DESCRIPTION:
Ballot's saucer scallop grows to a shell diameter of 12cm. The upper shell is reddish-brown with a pattern of concentric dark lines. The lower shell is chalky white.

HABITAT:
Coastal waters from Bowen (north Queensland) south along the Queensland coast to the New South Wales border.

A commercial fishery based in Gladstone and Bundaberg targets Ballot's saucer scallops.

DPI FISHERIES

Fan scallop

Marketing name: Scallop

Annachlamys flabellata

DESCRIPTION:

This species of fan scallop grows to about 8cm. They have the typical fan-like shape and fluted shell of commercial scallops of southern Australian waters, but are much smaller. Fan scallops are commonly pinkish-white, but colouration varies widely.

HABITAT:

Fan scallops range throughout Queensland coastal waters.

NOTES:

These scallops are taken as byproduct by trawlers and are infrequently marketed as fresh, unshucked "scallops".

DPI FISHERIES

Minimum Size: Nil.

Bag Limit: 50 molluscs taken or had in possession at any one time.

Ark cockle

Marketing name: Cockle

Anadara trapezia

DESCRIPTION:
Ark cockles grow to 7cm and have thick, oblique shells with predominant ridges. Colouration is creamy grey with brown margins where the shells meet.

HABITAT:
These cockles are found along the southern Queensland coastline from Fraser Island to the New South Wales border. They prefer estuarine tidal flats and seagrass beds.

NOTES:
Harvested by hand, ark cockles are occasionally marketed as fresh unshucked "cockles" for food.

It is illegal to remove oysters from any oyster ground.
However, a person may consume oysters "on the spot" in any
public oyster reserve or on unlicensed oyster grounds.

Commercial oyster
(Blacklip oyster, Milky oyster, Sydney rock oyster)

Marketing name: Oyster

Saccostrea commercialis

DESCRIPTION:
Commercial oysters grow to about 10cm. They have rough,
sharp-edged shells which are usually grey to black.

HABITAT:
Commercial oysters range through sheltered coastal
waters in Queensland south from about Gladstone to the
New South Wales border.

NOTES:
Commercial oysters occurred naturally in abundance in
south-east Queensland until about 1910. They were easily
collected by hand from banks of the intertidal zone or in
shallows at low tide, and also occurred as "dredge oysters"
in sub-tidal waters. As abundance dropped, a husbandry
industry grew and the commercial oyster is now cultivated
in specific areas on licensed oyster banks.

DPI FISHERIES

Minimum Size: Nil.

Bag Limit: 50 molluscs taken or had in possession at any one time.

Pipi
(Eugarie)

Marketing name: Pipi

Plebidonax deltoides

DESCRIPTION:
Pipis grow to 8cm. The wedge-shaped shells vary in colour from buff to pink or bluish-grey.

HABITAT:
Found mainly along the southern Queensland coast, pipis live in the shifting sands created by tides on ocean beaches.

NOTES:
Pipis may often be seen burrowing quickly into the sand along the surfline, immediately after a wave breaks on the sand. Pipis are used as bait for bream, whiting and dart.

DPI FISHERIES

Minimum Size: 6.2cm across the carapace.

Bag Limit: Nil.

Egg-bearing female Moreton Bay bugs and egg-bearing females of other sea bugs and slipper lobsters are totally protected in Queensland.

Moreton Bay bug
(Bay lobster, Shovelnose lobster, Gulf lobster)

Marketing name: Moreton Bay bug

Thenus orientalis

DESCRIPTION:

Moreton Bay bugs grow to a length of 28cm. They are brownish-red in colour with speckling and have dull yellowish tails. Their eyes are located at the outer edge of the carapace, a feature which distinguishes them from the related Balmain bug.

HABITAT:

Moreton Bay bugs are found throughout Queensland coastal waters, preferring sea beds of mud, sandy mud or rubble.

NOTES:

Moreton Bay bugs were discovered when otter trawling began in Moreton Bay in the 1950s. They are caught in trawl nets.

DPI FISHERIES

Minimum Size: 15cm (across the carapace).

Bag Limit: Nil (Males only). All females protected.

Blue swimmer crab
(Sand crab)

Marketing name: Blue swimmer crab

Portunus pelagicus

DESCRIPTION:
Blue swimmers grow to a shell breadth of about 20cm. Male crabs are blue or purple with pearly white mottling. Female crabs are not as colourful, being drab brown with pale mottling. Females are also smaller than males.

HABITAT:
Blue swimmers are found in estuaries, bays and shallow coastal areas along the Queensland coast. They prefer seabeds of sand, rubble or weed.

NOTES:
Female crabs can mate only after they moult, when their shells are soft and flexible. Fertile eggs are carried en-masse under the female's tail flap and she is said to be "berried".

Minimum Size: 15cm (across the carapace).
Bag Limit: 10 males (females protected).

Mud crab
(Mangrove crab)

Marketing name: Mud crab

Scylla **spp.**

DESCRIPTION:

Mud crabs grow to more than 25cm shell breadth (2kg), with males generally growing larger than females. Colouration varies from dark olive brown to greenish-blue and blue-black. Patterns of lighter-coloured dots cover the walking legs. Mud crabs have large and powerful claws used to crush shells.

HABITAT:

Mud crabs are found along the entire Queensland coast in sheltered estuaries, tidal flats and rivers lined with mangroves.

NOTES:

Mud crabs have an ability common to most crustaceans: they are able to "throw" a claw or leg if necessary to make a hasty retreat. These limbs eventually grow back, becoming larger and more developed with each successive moult.

FISH GUIDE

DPI FISHERIES: Egg-bearing female. INSET: Normal top view.

Minimum Size: 10cm (down the carapace).

Bag Limit: 20 males outside the closed season (November 20 to December 20). **Egg-bearing (berried) females are totally protected.**

Spanner crab
(Frog crab)

Marketing name: Spanner crab

Ranina ranina

DESCRIPTION:

Male spanner crabs grow to about 15cm shell breadth. Females grow only to about 11.5cm shell breadth. Spanner crabs are instantly recognisable by their frog-like appearance and bright red colouration. They derive their name from the spanner-shaped claws. A pattern of white dots is usually present across the middle of the carapace.

HABITAT:

Spanner crabs are found along the southern and central Queensland coast. They prefer sandy bottoms to about 40m.

NOTES:

While other crab species' shells turn red upon cooking, spanner crabs are red both cooked and uncooked. As with most crab species, the female spanner crab carries her eggs under her tail flap.

HOW TO DISTINGUISH THE SEX OF A CRAB

The male (*left above*) has a long, narrow flap on the underside. The female (*right above*) has a broad flap under which she carries her eggs.

CRAB POTS AND DILLIES IN TIDAL WATERS

Any person older than 15 years of age may use a maximum of four crab pots or dillies, in any combination, in tidal waters.

All pots and dillies must be marked by an identifying tag bearing the surname and address of the owner. When in use and not secured to a fixed object such as a jetty or anchored vessel, each pot or dilly must be attached to a light-coloured surface float (not less than 15cm in any dimension) with the name of its owner clearly inscribed on the float in a contrasting colour.

The hoop of a dilly net may be no larger than 125cm in diameter.

Canister traps may be no more than 60cm in length with a width, height or diameter of no more than 50cm.

Funnel traps may be no more than 70cm in length, with a height and/or width of no more than 50cm. They may have no more than four entrance holes no larger than 10cm in any dimension.

DPI FISHERIES

Minimum Size: Nil.   **Bag Limit: Nil.**

Amberjack
(Greater amberjack, Kingfish)

Seriola dumerili

DESCRIPTION:
Amberjack grow to at least 190cm (40kg) and are similar to yellowtail kingfish without any yellowish colour on the tail fin. Amberjack have a yellow band running the length of the body through the eye and to the tail.

HABITAT:
Amberjack may be found along the entire Queensland coast. Smaller fish shoal adjacent to inshore reefs. Larger fish tend to be solitary.

NOTES:
Amberjack are strong fighters which need to be chilled immediately upon capture.

The Queensland Fisheries Management Authority collects and analyses information about how, where, when and what we catch as part of its management and development of sustainable fish resources for our future.

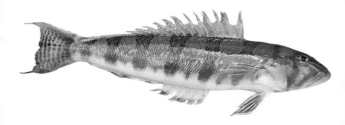

Minimum Size: Nil.

Bag Limit: Nil.

Bar-faced weever
(Rock whiting, Grubfish)

Parapercis nebulosus

DESCRIPTION:

Bar-faced weevers grow to 34cm. They are named for the blue lines that cross from the snout to the eyes. Their bodies are mottled vermillion (red) with darker vertical bands that are most prominent on the lower sides.

HABITAT:

Bar-faced weevers are found throughout Queensland coastal waters, on sandy bottoms near reefs and rocky outcrops.

Minimum Size: 58cm. Max.: 120cm.　　　　**Bag Limit: 5.**

Barramundi
(Giant perch)

Marketing name: Barramundi

Lates calcarifer

DESCRIPTION:

Barramundi are large predators able to adapt to either fresh or salt water. They are capable of forcing their way through nets using exposed, razor-sharp bones located near the base of each pectoral fin. Although they grow to 150cm (55kg), they are rarely caught over 30kg. They are greenish-bronze along the back, shading to silver along the sides, with white bellies. Young fish often have yellowish pelvic and tail fins. Juvenile barramundi have cream-coloured and dark blotches on their bodies, enabling them to be effectively camouflaged among snags and weeds of their natural habitat (*See Barramundi, Freshwater, Page 18*).

HABITAT:

Barramundi are found in freshwater lagoons, tidal rivers and estuaries from Maryborough to the Torres Strait and throughout the Gulf of Carpentaria. Adult fish spawn in coastal seas and estuaries.

NOTES:

Most barramundi begin their lives as males and change to females as they become much larger, hence the maximum legal size limit to protect mature females.

FISH GUIDE　　　　　　　　　　　　　　**51**

Minimum Size: Nil.   **Bag Limit: Nil.**

Happy moments spinefoot
(Black spinefoot, Stinging bream)

Marketing name: Black trevally

Siganus spinus

DESCRIPTION:
Happy moments grow to 35cm. Their bodies are olive brown with a network of fine bluish-white lines and scattered black spots (more prominent along the back at the base of the dorsal fin). There may be a dark smudge-spot behind the gill cover and a white bar at the base of the tail.

HABITAT:
Happy moments are found in coastal waters along the entire Queensland coast.

NOTES:
Spines along the dorsal fin and procumbent spine (a spine lying flat along the head, immediately in front of the dorsal fin) have venom glands that may inflict painful wounds. Some wounds may require medical attention, depending on the severity of the sting.

DPI FISHERIES

Minimum Size: 23cm.   **Bag Limit: Nil.**

Yellowfin bream
(Bream, Sea bream, Silver bream)

Marketing name: Yellowfin bream

Acanthopagrus australis

DESCRIPTION:
The yellowfin bream is one of Queensland's most popular estuarine angling species. It also accounts for a significant proportion of the commercial fresh fish market in southern Queensland. These fish vary in colour from bright silver to greyish green, but usually have yellow pelvic and anal fins (along the belly of the fish). Yellowfin bream may grow to 45cm (4kg). A black spot at the base of their pectoral fins distinguishes them from the pikey bream and tarwhine.

HABITAT:
Found predominantly from south-east Queensland to north Queensland, yellowfin are caught in estuaries, along surf beaches and off open headlands.

Minimum Size: 40cm.

DPI FISHERIES
Bag Limit: Nil.

Barramundi cod
(Humpback cod)

Marketing name: Barramundi cod

Cromileptes altivelis

DESCRIPTION:

Barramundi cod grow to 70cm (5kg) and are recognised by their profile and distinctive colouration. The creamy-grey head, body and fins are uniformly covered by well-spaced, dark brown to black dots. The small head and sharply rising nape are reminiscent of barramundi.

HABITAT:

Barramundi cod prefer reef environments along the Great Barrier Reef from the Capricorn-Bunker reef groups in central Queensland to the Torres Strait.

DPI FISHERIES

Minimum Size: Nil.

Bag Limit: Nil.

Black-tipped cod
(Footballer cod)

Marketing name: Rock cod

Epinephelus fasciatus

DESCRIPTION:
Black-tipped cod grow to about 40cm (1.2kg) and are dull red with brighter red vertical bars along their sides. The tips of their spiny dorsal fins are usually tipped with jet black. Colouration becomes less distinct with age and may not be as bright in more turbid waters.

HABITAT:
Black-tipped cod are found on coastal reefs along the Queensland coast.

Licences are not required for recreational fishing in Queensland. Regulations do limit minimum and maximum fish sizes and gender for some species, maximum number caught per trip and the fishing apparatus used. Regulations also control the closures of specific areas to fishing and seasonal closures for some species.

Minimum Size: Nil.

Bag Limit: Nil.

Coral cod
(Round-tailed cod)

Marketing name: Coral cod

Cephalopholis miniatus

DESCRIPTION:

Coral cod grow to about 50cm and may be either light or dark red with a profusion of blue spots on the head, body and fins. Sometimes confused with the coral trout because of similar colouration, coral cod have a rounded tail whereas coral trout have a wedge-shaped tail.

HABITAT:

Coral cod are found on reef slopes along the entire Great Barrier Reef, although they are more abundant in the state's northern waters.

DPI FISHERIES

Minimum Size: 35cm. Max.: 120cm.   **Bag Limit: 10.**

Estuary cod
(Goldspot cod, Orange spotted cod)

Marketing name: Rock cod

Epinephelus coioides (tauvina)

DESCRIPTION:
Although smaller than the Queensland groper, estuary cod can grow to 220cm (230kg). They have olive green or creamy brown body colouration, with profuse yellowish-orange or reddish-brown spots, extending on to most of the fins.

HABITAT:
Estuary cod are widespread along the Queensland coastline. Younger fish are commonly caught in estuaries.

NOTES:
These cod are sometimes found trapped in pots set out for mud crabs.

More than two-thirds of Queensland anglers (71.1%) fish saltwater only, 7.4% freshwater only and 21.5% fish both.
— Source: QFMA Recreational Fishing Survey 1997

Minimum Size: Nil.

DPI FISHERIES
Bag Limit: Nil.

Flowery cod

Marketing name: Rock cod

Epinephelus fuscoguttatus

DESCRIPTION:

Flowery cod grow to 10kg. The dark brown blotches on the sides of these fish vary in number and pattern, but are characteristic of the species.

HABITAT:

Found along the Queensland coast, flowery cod inhabit coral reefs, rocky foreshores and, occasionally, mangrove-lined creeks and rivers.

NOTES:

Adult fish are typically line-fished over coral reefs.

Minimum Size: Nil.

Bag Limit: Nil.

Honeycomb cod
(Birdwire cod, Wire netting cod)

Marketing name: Rock cod

Epinephelus merra

DESCRIPTION:

Honeycomb cod grow to about 45cm with colouration ranging from creamy white to yellowish brown. Spots covering the body are vaguely hexagonal, resembling honeycomb. These spots are darker brown. Similar to the long-finned cod, the honeycomb cod can be distinguished by having shorter pectoral fins lacking a creamy blotch at the base, bisected by a brown bar.

HABITAT:

Honeycomb cod are widespread throughout Queensland coastal waters and the Great Barrier Reef, often sheltering beneath dead coral clumps.

NOTES:

Sharp dorsal spines and sharp-edged gill covers require careful handling as they may inflict painful injuries.

DPI FISHERIES

Minimum Size: Nil.

Bag Limit: Nil.

Long-finned cod

Marketing name: Rock cod

Epinephelus quoyanus

DESCRIPTION:

Long-finned cod grow to 45cm, but are commonly caught at 35cm. Resembling honeycomb cod, the long-finned cod have similar markings but have much larger and darker pectoral fins. The pectoral fins also are marked with a creamy-ivory coloured patch at their base, bisected by a brown bar.

HABITAT:

Long-finned cod are common in reef waters around the Queensland coast, north from the Capricorn-Bunker reef groups.

NOTES:

Long-finned cod are surprisingly quick over short distances, belying their apparently cumbersome shape.

Minimum Size: Nil.   **Bag Limit: Nil.**

Maori cod

Marketing name: Rock cod

Epinephelus undulostriatus

DESCRIPTION:
Maori cod grow to 50cm (5.5kg). Colouration is rich brown to creamy brown, with intricately patterned rust or orange-red lines covering the body. The soft dorsal, anal and tail fins are deeply edged with bright yellow.

HABITAT:
In Queensland, Maori cod inhabit reef waters from the Capricorn-Bunker reef groups in central Queensland to the New South Wales border.

NOTES:
Maori cod will often dart from their hiding places to snatch food from the surface, only to dart back just as quickly.

Minimum Size: 35cm. Max.: 120cm.   **Bag Limit: 1.**

Potato cod

Marketing name: Rock cod

Epinephelus tukula

DESCRIPTION:

Although very similar to Queensland groper, the potato cod exhibits typical colouring of creamy white with black blotches over the body. More linear blotches radiate outwards from the eye. When potato cod are captured, the creamy white darkens to exhibit colouring similar to the groper, hence it is often mistaken as the latter fish. Potato cod grow to more than 90kg.

HABITAT:

Originally thought to occur only in an isolated spot at Cormorant Pass (near Lizard Island in far north Queensland), potato cod are found throughout the northern waters of the Great Barrier Reef.

NOTES:

Potato cod are large, inoffensive and fearless, but may become demanding when they are being hand-fed, when they may mistake hands for offered food.

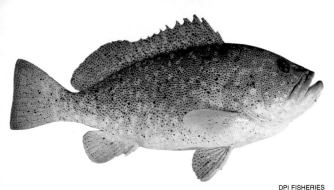

DPI FISHERIES

Minimum Size: Nil. **Bag Limit: Nil.**

Purple cod

Marketing name: Rock cod

Epinephelus flavocaeruleus

DESCRIPTION:
Purple cod are immediately different from other cod in their blue body colouration (a feature they share with blue Maori cod). Colouration may vary from pale blue or lilac through to deep blue-purple. Black spots cover the body. Purple cod grow to 90cm.

HABITAT:
Purple cod are found in reef waters in the northern sector of the Great Barrier Reef.

NOTES:
Purple cod are distinguished from blue Maori cod in having bright yellow to orange fins.

DPI FISHERIES

Minimum Size: Nil. **Bag Limit: Nil.**

Tomato cod

Marketing name: Coral cod

Cephalopholis sonnerati

DESCRIPTION:
Growing to about 65cm, the tomato cod are bright orange-red. Small darker red spots cover the head and body, and lighter coloured bands may be present towards the tail.

HABITAT:
They are found extensively in reef areas along the Queensland coast from Cape Moreton in the south to the Gulf of Carpentaria.

NOTES:
Light bands on the tail-end of these fish are present only in live specimens.

DPI FISHERIES

Minimum Size: Nil.   **Bag Limit: Nil.**

Yellow-spotted cod

Marketing name: Rock cod

Epinephelus areolatus

DESCRIPTION:
Yellow-spotted cod grow to 60cm or more. Their creamy brown bodies are covered with golden spots which darken on the fins. The tail fin has a white margin along the trailing edge.

HABITAT:
Yellow-spotted cod are found in reef waters in the northern part of Queensland.

NOTES:
Yellow-spotted cod are distinct from estuary cod (gold-spot cod) in having a squared-off tail with a white border (rather than a rounded tail).

Commercial fishing is the fifth largest primary industry in Queensland.

Minimum Size: Nil. **Bag Limit: Nil.**

Snub-nosed dart
(Snubnose dart, Oyster-eater)

Marketing name: Dart

Trachinotus blochi

DESCRIPTION:

Snub-nosed dart are reported to grow to 86cm and weights of 9.3kg. They are silvery-grey fish with dark fins. Young fish have long, swept-back, black fins. Adult fish lack the extended fins of juveniles and are more rounded in shape. The anal fins are yellowish-orange with black tips, helping to distinguish the young of this species from the giant oyster cracker.

HABITAT:

Snub-nosed dart range throughout Queensland's coastal waters, including bays and estuaries, from Fraser Island north.

NOTES:

Snub-nosed dart have specialised teeth formed into hard plates which are used for crushing molluscs.

FISH GUIDE

DPI FISHERIES

Minimum Size: Nil.   **Bag Limit: Nil.**

Southern swallowtail dart
(Surf trevally, Large-spotted dart)

Marketing name: Dart

Trachinotus botla

DESCRIPTION:
Southern swallowtail dart are usually caught at about 1kg and are silvery fish with several thumbprint-sized blotches along the side above the lateral line.

HABITAT:
Southern swallowtail are found in surf waters along the southern and central Queensland coast.

NOTES:
Swallowtail dart form into shoals that move along the surfline. They provide excellent sport for surf fishing.

DPI FISHERIES

Minimum Size: 45cm.

Bag Limit: Nil.

Dolphin fish

(Mahi-mahi, Dorado)

Coryphaena hippurus

DESCRIPTION:

Growing to 163cm (22.4kg), dolphinfish have long, deep, flat bodies which are blue along the back and yellow below, with black speckling. Colours of freshly caught fish change dramatically before death. The male dolphinfish develop steep head profiles as they age. This feature is less distinctive in females. Both sexes have long dorsal fins that extend from head to tail.

HABITAT:

Considered more of a sportfish, dolphinfish range along the Queensland coast in open water.

NOTES:

Groups of dolphinfish sometimes congregate under pieces of flotsam in open water.

Minimum Size: 45cm.   **Bag Limit: 10.**

Red emperor
(Government bream)

Marketing name: Red emperor

Lutjanus sebae

DESCRIPTION:
Red emperor grow to more than 22kg, although they are more commonly caught at 10kg or less. The typical red banding forming an "arrow" shape at the middle of the body is more distinct in younger fish, and may fade with death. Red emperor have a prominent "U"-shaped notch in the foremost cleft of the gill cover which distinguishes them from large-mouth nannygai which have only a slight indentation.

HABITAT:
Red emperor are widely distributed on rocky and coralline reefs along the entire Queensland coast.

FISH GUIDE   69

DPI FISHERIES

Minimum Size: 35cm.

Bag Limit: 10.

Red throat emperor
(Red throat sweetlip, Tricky snapper, Lipper)

Marketing name: Emperor

Lethrinus miniatus

DESCRIPTION:

Red throat emperor grow to more than 90cm. They have a dorsal spiny fin which is mostly, if not entirely, bright red as are the pectoral and pelvic fins at their base. The inside of the mouth and throat is also red. Although the body colour of freshly caught fish is typically reddish brown with darker cross bars, colouration may fade to silver upon death.

HABITAT:

Red throat emperor are commonly caught in coastal and reef waters from Moreton Bay in the south, northwards along the Queensland coast.

DPI FISHERIES

Minimum Size: 40cm.

Bag Limit: 10.

Spangled emperor
(Yellow sweetlip)

Marketing name: Emperor

Lethrinus nebulosus

DESCRIPTION:
Spangled emperor grow to more than 90cm (10kg). Colouration is yellow to yellowy-olive, with scales along the back and upper sides having a pearly blue central mark that produces a spangled effect. The lower sides are pale with faint yellow lines marking the scale rows. The snout, nape and cheeks are streaked with silvery-blue, and the upper parts of the pectoral fins are blue.

HABITAT:
Spangled emperor are found along the entire Queensland coast, preferring sandy seabeds next to reefs.

Keeping track of Queensland's fish stocks is not as simple as walking out into the paddock and counting the cows.

DPI FISHERIES

Minimum Size: 30cm.

Bag Limit: Nil.

Bartail flathead
(Flagtail flathead)

Marketing name: Bartail flathead

Platycephalus indicus

DESCRIPTION:

Bartail flathead grow to at least 80cm, but are more commonly caught much smaller. The pattern of the "flag" on the tail is characteristic of bartail flathead — bright white with three distinct black bars crossing horizontally. There is a yellow patch on the tail, also distinctive of the species.

HABITAT:

Bartail flathead prefer sandy bottoms in inshore waters along most of the Queensland coastline.

NOTES:

Two species of bartail flathead are found in Queensland — *Platycephalus indicus* and *Platycephalus endrachtensis*. They are almost identical except for the placement of the yellow colouration on the tail: *P. indicus* has the yellow in the middle of the tail and *P. endrachtensis* has yellow on the upper edge of the tail. Care should be taken when handling flathead to avoid injury from the sharp spines.

Minimum Size: 30cm.   **Bag Limit: Nil.**

Dusky flathead
(Mud flathead)

Marketing name: Dusky flathead

Platycephalus fuscus

DESCRIPTION:
Dusky flathead are large fish growing to 15kg. Dusky flathead living over clean, sandy bottoms are brown in colour, changing to mottled green and brown in those fish living near seagrass beds. Dusky flathead are distinguished by a black spot on their tails, partially bordered with white.

HABITAT:
Dusky flathead range along the southern and central Queensland coast to Mackay in the north. They are found along ocean beaches, in bays, estuaries and coastal rivers.

NOTES:
Dusky flathead are one of Queensland's most important angling species.

DPI FISHERIES

Minimum Size: 30cm.

Bag Limit: Nil.

Sand flathead

Marketing name: Northern sand flathead

Platycephalus arenarius

DESCRIPTION:

Sand flathead grow to 45cm (5kg). Colouration is creamy to sandy brown, covered in fawn to rusty speckling, graduating to a white belly. Sand flathead have distinctive tails which are white with oblique black bars. The lowest two bars are generally thicker than the others.

HABITAT:

Sand flathead are found along the entire Queensland coast, on sandy bottoms along beaches and estuaries.

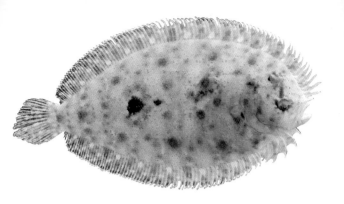

Minimum Size: Nil.   **Bag Limit: Nil.**

Flounder

Marketing name: Flounder (various species)

Various

DESCRIPTION:

Flounder belong to a group of fishes known as flatfishes and are distinctive in their shape. While flatfishes begin their lives as "normal", bilaterally symmetrical fish, their bodies change dramatically as they grow — one eye "migrating" over to the same side as the other, and the side where that eye came from becomes the bottom of the fish as it lies on the sea bed. This "underside" becomes creamy or white, while the "topside" develops colouration typical to each separate species of flatfish.

HABITAT:

Flounder are found along the entire Queensland coast, generally over sandy bottoms from deeper areas (about 70m) to bays and estuaries.

NOTES:

Flounder are usually caught as bycatch in trawl nets. Some, such as the large-toothed flounder and small-toothed flounder, are occasionally taken by recreational anglers.

DPI FISHERIES

Minimum Size: Nil.

Bag Limit: Nil.

Three-by-two garfish
(Flat-sided garfish)

Marketing name: Northern garfish

Hemiramphus robustus

DESCRIPTION:

Three-by-two garfish grow to 46cm. They are readily distinguished from other garfish in their angular shape and the presence of a black spot directly below their dorsal fin. Colouration is blue-green along the back with silvery sides. A broad silvery band runs along the sides. The upper lobe of the tail is yellow, bordered with black.

HABITAT:

Three-by-two garfish are found along the entire Queensland coast, inhabiting bays, estuaries, coastal reef areas and lagoons of the Great Barrier Reef.

DPI FISHERIES

Minimum Size: Nil.   **Bag Limit: Nil.**

River garfish
(Needle gar, Splinter gar)

Marketing name: River garfish

Hyporhamphus ardelio

DESCRIPTION:
Growing to about 38cm, river garfish are green along the back and silvery below. They have a broad silvery band running along the length of their bodies. Two to three thin, dark lines run along the upper sides. River garfish have long, slender beaks tipped with orange. River garfish are distinguished from Eastern sea garfish by the shape of their upper beak — it is much wider than it is long. In Eastern sea garfish, the upper beak is always as long as it is wide.

HABITAT:
River garfish occur along the southern Queensland coast from Gladstone south. They are found in tidal rivers, estuaries, bays and coastal waters over seagrass beds.

NOTES:
River garfish are important recreational and commercial fish, taken by anglers, gill, seine, tunnel and cast nets.

Ninety-five percent of Queensland households eat seafood at least once a year.

DPI FISHERIES

Minimum Size: Nil.

Bag Limit: Nil.

Snub-nosed garfish
(Short-bill, Snubbie)

Marketing name: Northern garfish

Arrhamphus sclerolepis

DESCRIPTION:

Snub-nosed garfish grow to about 40cm. Colouration is green along the back with silvery lower sides and belly. As with other garfish, an obvious silvery line runs along the length of the long, slender body from the pectoral fin to the tail. Snub-nosed garfish have a stouter body than most other garfish and are easily identifiable by the short lower, red-tipped beak which barely extends past the upper jaw.

HABITAT:

Snub-nosed garfish are found along the entire Queensland coastline, preferring shallow waters over seagrass beds. They are also found in freshwater dams and lakes.

Minimum Size: 30cm.   **Bag Limit: Nil.**

Spotted grunter bream
(Small spotted grunter bream)

Marketing name: Grunter

Pomadasys argenteus

DESCRIPTION:
Spotted grunter bream are important recreational and commercial food fish, growing to about 50cm (5kg). Often confused with barred grunter bream, spotted grunter bream have small black to brown spots which are scattered over the upper sides of the fish. These spots do not form bar-shaped patterns as with the spots of the barred grunter bream. The ventral and anal fins are tinged with yellow.

HABITAT:
Spotted grunter bream are found along the entire Queensland coast, although they prefer tropical latitudes where they inhabit mangrove-lined rivers and coastal flats.

Minimum. Size: 30cm (Qld east coast)
40cm (Gulf of Carpentaria).
Bag Limit: 20 (Gulf of Carpentaria).

Barred grunter bream
(Spotted grunter bream)

Marketing name: Grunter

Pomadasys kaakan

DESCRIPTION:
Barred grunter bream grow to at least 6kg. The pattern of bars on the sides of these fish is made up of brown spots. The intensity of these spots may increase or decrease with mood and disappear with death. Barred grunter bream may be distinguished from the spotted grunter bream in having a white margin along the tip of the lower lobe of the tail fin (the spotted grunter bream has a margin which is more creamy yellow).

HABITAT:
Barred grunter bream may be found in coastal waters and estuaries along the Queensland coast.

Minimum Size: 25cm.   **Bag Limit: Nil.**

Hussar

Marketing name: Hussar

Lutjanus adetii

DESCRIPTION:

Hussar grow to about 50cm, but are more commonly caught at 30cm. These fish are brightly coloured — bright rosy pink above, shading to pinkish-white on the belly. A broad, bright yellow band extends from the gill cover behind the eye to the base of the tail. The eyes are ringed with red and yellow, the yellow extending along the nose. The pink ventral and anal fins have bright white leading edges, and the dorsal and caudal (tail) fins are edged in red.

HABITAT:

Hussar range from about Stradbroke Island in southern Queensland to Princess Charlotte Bay in north Queensland. These fish prefer rocky and coralline reefs, although large shoals of hussar appear over rubble seabeds.

NOTES:

This abundant fish is taken by line fishing along rocky mainland shores, around islands and adjacent reefs. Hussars form extensive shoals that may dominate your catch when you are seeking other reef species.

DPI FISHERIES

Minimum Size: 75cm.   **Bag Limit: 10.**

Black kingfish
(Cobia, Crab-eater)

Marketing name: Black kingfish

Rachycentron canadus

DESCRIPTION:
Black kingfish are large fish growing to more than 200cm (60kg). They have flattened heads and long, streamlined bodies. Colouration is dark brown to black along the back with one or two indistinct ribbons of grey along the sides. The belly is usually dull yellow.

HABITAT:
Preferring reef habitats, black kingfish range along the entire Queensland coast.

NOTES:
Black kingfish may sometimes travel in small groups under large manta rays, and may be caught by trolling bait near large buoys or beacons.

DPI FISHERIES

Minimum Size: 50cm.   **Bag Limit: Nil.**

Yellowtail kingfish
(King amberjack)

Marketing name: Yellowtail kingfish

Seriola lalandi

DESCRIPTION:
Yellowtail kingfish grow to more than 200cm (58kg). They are a large and powerful fish which provide excellent sport. Colouration is purple-blue along the back and upper flanks, and silver on the belly. These two colours are separated sharply by a brassy-yellow ribbon. The tail is distinctly yellow.

HABITAT:
Yellowtail kingfish range throughout Queensland waters, but are more commonly caught in southern Queensland. They gather near rocky headlands and deepwater jetties, over inshore reefs and seamounts.

NOTES:
Smaller fish (up to 7kg) congregate in shoals and may be enticed to the surface with chopped fish.

The Queensland Fisheries Management Authority organises and conducts public meetings throughout Queensland communities to discuss local problems and jointly seek solutions for the future.

Minimum Size: Nil.   **Bag Limit: Nil.**

Fan-bellied leatherjacket
(Pigfish)

Marketing name: Leatherjacket

Monacanthus chinensis

DESCRIPTION:

Fan-bellied leatherjackets are creamy green-brown fish, with large mottled patches of brown or black and intricate lacy tendrils of cream covering the body. They grow to 25cm. The tail has three brown vertical bars and often has fine blue lines along the outer edge. As the name suggests, the pelvic flap (near the belly) is unusually large and fan-shaped. Fine blue spots and bars extend along the outer rim of the pelvic flap and continue to the snout.

HABITAT:

Fan-bellied leatherjackets may be found along the east coast of Queensland, in estuaries and inlets.

NOTES:

Fan-bellied leatherjackets are notorious bait thieves. Owing to a large, erect spine on the heads, these fish are difficult to remove from nets.

Minimum Size: Nil.   **Bag Limit: Nil.**

Yellow-finned leatherjacket
(Yellow-tailed leatherjacket, Triggerfish)

Marketing name: Leatherjacket

Meuschenia trachylepis

DESCRIPTION:
Yellow-finned leatherjackets grow to 40cm (1kg) and have a dorsal spine which can be locked into position (a feature common in leatherjackets). Colouration is grey or brownish with yellow fins and olive brown blotches along the body. An intricate pattern of blue dots and bars may be present along the belly of the fish, depending on mood.

HABITAT:
Yellow-finned leatherjackets are found in southern Queensland from about Fraser Island, south. They prefer shallow coastal seas, bays and estuaries.

NOTES:
Yellow-finned leatherjackets are usually taken by nets and traps, and occasionally by recreational anglers. They are notorious bait thieves.

FISH GUIDE   **85**

DPI FISHERIES

Minimum Size: Nil.

Bag Limit: Nil.

Stout longtom

Tylosurus gavialoides

DESCRIPTION:

Stout longtom grow to about 130cm. They are greenish-black along the back, becoming white on the belly. Stout longtom have long, thick bodies and small sharp teeth in a slightly rounded beak.

HABITAT:

Stout longtom are found along the entire Queensland coast.

DPI FISHERIES

Minimum Size: 23cm.   **Bag Limit: Nil.**

Luderick
(Blackfish, Black bream)

Marketing name: Luderick

Girella tricuspidata

DESCRIPTION:
Luderick live in river mouths, estuaries, off ocean beaches near rocky outcrops and rock walls. Estuary species tend to be dark olive brown with dark, narrow, vertical bars on their bodies and a purplish tinge (which fades with death). Luderick from more open waters are paler with silvery bellies and their bodies have a bronze sheen. The dark bars on these ocean fish are more pronounced. Individual fish may move between habitats. Luderick grow to 71cm (5kg) but are usually caught at 0.6kg to 0.9kg.

HABITAT:
Luderick are more southerly fish, inhabiting sheltered bays and estuaries, and congregating adjacent to near-shore rocky outcrops. They range from Fraser Island to south of the New South Wales border.

NOTES:
Luderick are usually herbivores (plant-eating). Marine weed (algae) is used for bait. They may be enticed by yabbies.

FISH GUIDE   87

DPI FISHERIES

Minimum Size: 50cm.   **Bag Limit: 10.**

Grey mackerel
(Broad-barred mackerel, Tiger mackerel)

Marketing name: Grey mackerel

Scomberomorus semifasciatus

DESCRIPTION:

Usually caught at 2.3kg, grey mackerel can grow to 8kg. They are distinct from other mackerel in having a deeper body, a black first dorsal fin and wide bars along their sides. These bars fade upon capture and death. Colouration is pale green along the back with silvery sides, which fades upon death to dull grey.

HABITAT:

Grey mackerel are found along all of the Queensland coast, becoming more common in major bays.

DPI FISHERIES

Minimum Size: 50cm.   **Bag Limit: 30.**

School mackerel
(Doggie mackerel)

Marketing name: School mackerel

Scomberomorus queenslandicus

DESCRIPTION:

School mackerel grow to 130cm (12kg) but are more commonly caught at 2.3kg. Although similar to the spotted mackerel (*Scomberomorus munroi*), school mackerel are distinguished by having fewer, less distinct spots over the body, and a dorsal fin with a distinct white patch. Colouration along the back is blue-green over a bright silvery-white body.

HABITAT:

School mackerel are found along the entire Queensland coast.

NOTES:

In southern Queensland, and particularly in Moreton Bay, large feeding shoals move into the bay during winter and spring, providing excellent fishing for both recreational anglers and professionals alike.

One third of Queensland householders go recreational fishing, crabbing or prawning at least once a year.
— Source: QFMA Recreational Fishing Survey 1997

DPI FISHERIES

Minimum Size: 50cm.   **Bag Limit: Nil.**

Shark mackerel
(Scaly mackerel, Salmon mackerel)

Marketing name: Shark mackerel

Grammatorcynus bicarinatus

DESCRIPTION:
Shark mackerel grow to a recorded length of 130cm (nearly 12kg). Colouration is pale yellowish green along the back and upper sides, shading to brassy-silver along the belly. In common with the big-eyed shark mackerel (*Grammatorcynus bilineatus*), shark mackerel have a secondary lateral line that loops downward from just behind the pectoral fin and rejoins the primary lateral line near the tail. Shark mackerel usually have a series of dark spots along the breast and belly.

HABITAT:
Found all along the Queensland coast, shark mackerel prefer waters adjacent to coral reefs.

NOTES:
Shark mackerel, when gutted, exude a distinct smell of ammonia.

Minimum Size: 75cm.   **Bag Limit: 10.**

Spanish mackerel
(Narrow-barred mackerel, Blue mackerel)

Marketing name: Spanish mackerel

Scomberomorus commerson

DESCRIPTION:
Spanish mackerel are the largest of the Queensland mackerel, growing to 220cm (60kg), but are more commonly caught at 7kg to 10kg. They are irridescent blue-green along their backs and upper sides, shading to silvery-grey on the belly. A distinguishing feature is that Spanish mackerel have numerous, narrow, wavy, vertical lines along their sides, the number of which increases with the fish's size.

HABITAT:
Preferring reef waters and rocky headlands, Spanish mackerel may be found all along the Queensland coast.

NOTES:
Smaller fish (7kg to 10kg) form great shoals which are targeted by commercial fishermen. Large fish (more than 27kg) are generally solitary.

Current consultative processes between Queensland's administrators and the State's population, which enable the people to decide which regulations they want, are recognised as a leading model in natural resource management.

Minimum Size: 35cm.   **Bag Limit: Nil.**

Mangrove Jack
(Dog bream, Red bream, Reef red bream)

Marketing name: Sea perch

Lutjanus argentimaculatus

DESCRIPTION:
Mangrove Jack may reach weights of up to 16kg, but are usually caught around 5.5kg. Young fish are uniformly reddish-brown or copper coloured, becoming paler in reef waters and often with a pearly mark in the centre of each scale. Colour may vary, reflecting the fish's habitat, that is, reef fish tend to be lighter and brighter in colour compared to fish caught in estuaries.

HABITAT:
Mangrove Jack are widely distributed in both estuarine and reef waters along the Queensland coast and the Great Barrier Reef. Young fish occupy estuaries and rivers to the extent of tidal influence, moving seaward to reef waters by the time they have grown to 3kg.

NOTES:
Mangrove Jack are energetic fighters.

Minimum Size: 75cm.   **Bag Limit: 1.**

Hump-headed Maori wrasse
(Giant wrasse, Napoleon)

Marketing name: Maori wrasse

Cheilinus undulatus

DESCRIPTION:
Hump-headed Maori wrasse are very large fish growing to 230cm (about 190kg), but are more commonly seen at 50kg. They have thick, fleshy lips and a hump that forms on the head above the eyes, becoming more prominent with age. The cheeks display an intricate pattern of wavy lines, bordered above by a distinctive black and brown line that is horizontal behind the eye and slants down to the upper jaw. The greenish-brown scales are bordered with creamy white and are extremely large (sometimes more than 10cm in diameter).

HABITAT:
Hump-headed Maori wrasse inhabit waters of the Great Barrier Reef north to Papua New Guinea.

NOTES:
Maori wrasse have large, peg-like teeth which they use to crush coral and shells in order to feed on burrowing worms and molluscs.

Minimum Size: Nil. **Bag Limit: Nil.**

Violet-lined Maori wrasse

Cheilinus diagrammus

DESCRIPTION:

Growing to 38cm, violet-lined Maori wrasse have oblique violet lines on the lower half of the head, which form an intricate pattern of lines and dots covering the head. The lower halves of their bodies, including the anal fin, range from pink to red. The tail fin is lemon yellow with dark fin rays.

HABITAT:

In Queensland, violet-lined Maori wrasse range throughout Great Barrier reef waters northwards through Torres Strait and westward to the Northern Territory.

Minimum Size: Nil.   **Bag Limit: Nil.**

Brown fatlip bream
(Morwong, Brown blubberlips, Blubberlip bream)

Plectorhinchus gibbosus

DESCRIPTION:
Some brown fatlip bream have lips so thick they look malformed. These fish grow to about 12kg, but are more commonly caught at 2kg to 3kg. Colouration is uniformly grey to brown with dark fins.

HABITAT:
Brown fatlip bream are found all along the Queensland coast. They prefer tidal rivers, estuaries and rubble seabeds adjacent to reefs.

NOTES:
The brown fatlip bream is rarely caught by anglers.

Minimum Size: 30cm.   **Bag Limit: Nil.**

Sea mullet
(Hardgut mullet, River mullet)

Marketing name: Sea mullet

Mugil cephalus

DESCRIPTION:

Sea mullet grow to more than 79cm (8kg), but are more commonly caught at about 2.5kg. Colouration varies, depending on the habitat the fish are taken from. In oceanic waters, sea mullet have olive-green backs and silvery sides. In river and estuaries, colouration is brownish along the back and silvery-grey on the sides. Sea mullet are robust with small, flattened heads, large eyes and fleshy lips.

HABITAT:

Found in coastal waters throughout Queensland, sea mullet are more abundant in the southern part of the State. They can be found in bays, estuaries, tidal rivers and on-shore waters. Younger fish often move into coastal rivers.

NOTES:

Sea mullet are targeted by commercial fishermen in south-east Queensland, and form the basis of a major fishery. Each year, mature fish group into large shoals and move up the coast on their annual spawning migration.

Minimum Size: 45cm.
Bag Limit: 10.

Mulloway
(Jewfish, Kingfish, School Jew)

Marketing name: Mulloway

Argyrosomus hololepidotus

DESCRIPTION:
Mulloway grow to about 180cm (60kg) but are more commonly caught at 7kg or more. Mulloway are silvery with an opalescent sheen, and pearly spots along the lateral line which fade with death. A black spot at the base of the pectoral fin is a distinguishing feature.

HABITAT:
Mulloway are found along the southern Queensland coast from Bundaberg south. They inhabit open ocean beaches, bays and rivers, preferring deeper water.

NOTES:
Small mulloway, commonly called school Jew, congregate in estuaries.

Up to six hooks per line are permitted when fishing tidal waters, but no more than three lines per person are allowed when fishing from a vessel.

DPI FISHERIES

Minimum Size: 40cm.

Bag Limit: 10.

Large-mouth nannygai
(Large-mouth red Jew, Large-mouth sea perch, Red Jew)

Marketing name: Sea perch

Lutjanus malabaricus

DESCRIPTION:

Large-mouth nannygai grow to 14kg or more. Their body colouration is a bright, glowing red, graduating to a dark pink on the belly. Large-mouth nannygai are similar to small-mouth nannygai in having a black spot "saddling" the base of the tail. They are different to small-mouth nannygai in having larger mouths and slightly concave head profiles.

HABITAT:

Large-mouth nannygai are found in the same areas as the small-mouth nannygai — in deeper reef waters from Cape Moreton north.

NOTES:

Large-mouth nannygai are easily confused with red emperor — the black tail spot is never present in red emperor.

DPI FISHERIES

Minimum Size: 40cm.   **Bag Limit: 10.**

Small-mouth nannygai
(Small-mouth red Jew, Small-mouth sea perch)

Marketing name: Sea perch

Lutjanus erythropterus

DESCRIPTION:
Small-mouth nannygai grow to around 10kg. Colouration is from bronze-red to bright red, with larger fish generally displaying darker colours. Both the small-mouth and large-mouth nannygai have a black spot on the dorsal surface of the tail base. Small-mouth nannygai differ from large-mouth nannygai in having smaller mouths and straighter head profiles.

HABITAT:
Small-mouth nannygai are found along the Queensland coast from Cape Moreton north, preferring deeper reef waters.

NOTES:
Small-mouth and large-mouth nannygai are commonly found together in mixed schools.

Minimum Size: Nil.

Bag Limit: Nil.

Blue-barred parrot fish

Marketing name: Parrot fish

Scarus ghobban

DESCRIPTION:
Blue-barred parrot fish grow to about 100cm and are one of the largest of the parrot fish family. Adult males and females display distinctly different colouration. Both sexes have orange heads with short blue bars radiating from their eyes and around their mouths, and yellow-orange bodies, but the males have more blue-green colouration on the scales, forming short bars. The bars on females are less distinct. In both sexes, the dorsal, anal and pelvic fins are bright yellow to yellow-orange, bordered by blue.

HABITAT:
Blue-barred parrot fish inhabit reef waters from the southern end of the Great Barrier Reef north.

NOTES:
Very few parrot fish are caught by anglers. Blue-barred parrot fish are one of these. Parrot fish are similar to tusk fish, but are easily distinguished by their teeth — tusk fish have separate, fang-like teeth, whereas the teeth of parrot fish are fused together to form a "beak".

FISH GUIDE

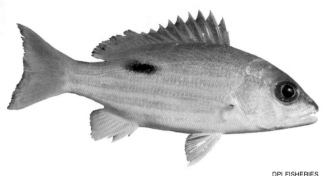

Minimum Size: Nil.   **Bag Limit: Nil.**

Black-spot sea perch
(Moses perch, Striped Moses perch)

Marketing name: Sea perch

Lutjanus fulviflamma

DESCRIPTION:
Black-spot sea perch grow to 50cm. They are slender fish with a flush of pink on the head graduating to a yellow body. The belly is white. A series of horizontal golden lines extend along the body from behind the eyes to the bright yellow tail. All the other fins are also bright yellow. Although black-spot sea perch have a black mark similar to that on the Moses perch, it differs in that it lies mostly below the lateral line.

HABITAT:
Black-spot sea perch prefer reef waters along the Queensland coast from the Tropic of Capricorn (central Queensland) north.

NOTES:
Black-spot sea perch are mostly taken by anglers on shallow coastal reefs and occasionally by trawlers.

DPI FISHERIES

Minimum Size: 25cm.   **Bag Limit: Nil.**

Moses perch
(Black-spot sea perch, Fingermark bream)

Marketing name: Sea perch

Lutjanus russelli

DESCRIPTION:
Moses perch grow to about 53cm (2kg) but are more commonly caught at 28cm to 38cm. They vary in colour from rosy pink to silvery white, with a prominent black spot or blotch above the lateral line and below the junction of the spiny and soft dorsal fins. There may also be a number of fine yellowish lines marking the scale rows along the sides.

HABITAT:
Moses perch are found along the entire Queensland coast. They occupy estuaries, bays and rocky coastal reefs, to offshore coral reefs.

Minimum Size: 30cm.   **Bag Limit: 10.**

Pearl perch

Marketing name: Pearl perch

Glaucosoma scapulare

DESCRIPTION:
Pearl perch grow to 70cm (7kg) but are usually caught at 30cm to 45cm. Colouration is silvery with a pale blue sheen. A dark spot may be present at the base of the soft dorsal fin. Pearl perch have a distinctive large eye, presumably owing to the fact that they feed mostly at night.

HABITAT:
Pearl perch are more southerly fish, inhabiting rocky and coralline reefs in Queensland from Rockhampton (central Queensland) to the New South Wales border.

NOTES:
These fish derive their name from a large, flattened bone located at the upper edge of the gill cover. This bone is usually covered by a delicate, black membrane which is easily damaged and removed, exposing the pearly-white bone.

DPI FISHERIES

Minimum Size: 25cm.

Bag Limit: Nil.

Stripey sea perch
(Stripey, Spanish flag)

Marketing name: Sea perch

Lutjanus carponotatus

DESCRIPTION:

Stripey sea perch grow to about 55cm. They are easily identified by horizontal golden lines running the length of their silvery bodies, from their eyes to their tails. All fins are yellow, becoming more orange-yellow on the dorsal and caudal (tail) fins. A black or dark brown spot is always present at the base of the pectoral fin.

HABITAT:

Stripey sea perch are widely distributed in Queensland waters from Moreton Bay north. They live in reef waters, around rocky outcrops and headlands, along the coast and the Great Barrier Reef.

Minimum Size: Nil. **Bag Limit: Nil.**

Giant queenfish
(Giant leatherskin, Giant dart, White-fish, Skinnyfish)

Marketing name: Queenfish

Scomberoides commersonianus

DESCRIPTION:
Giant queenfish grow to more than 120cm (14kg) and are powerful, swift pelagic fish. They are silvery-grey in colour with bronze patches on the head and dorsal surface. Live fish have a series of silvery spots along their sides above the lateral line, which become dusky with death.

HABITAT:
In Queensland, giant queenfish are found as far south as Fraser Island and are distributed north along the coast.

**The Queensland Industry of Recreational Fishing (QIRF)
is working with government bodies on fisheries
planning and development to ensure the future of
recreational angling. Membership ranges from the
proprietors of bait and tackle shops to the major
manufacturers of rods, reels and tackle.
Contact: QIRF, P.O. Box 6319, Acacia Ridge Qld 4110.**

FISH GUIDE 105

Minimum Size: Nil.   **Bag Limit: Nil.**

Skinny queenfish
(Queenfish)

Marketing name: Queenfish

Scomberoides lysan

DESCRIPTION:
Skinny queenfish grow to 80cm (5kg) and are similar to giant queenfish in appearance. These fish may be distinguished from the giant queenfish by the double row of spots along their flanks — one row above the lateral line, and one row below.

HABITAT:
Skinny queenfish are a tropical species, ranging along the Queensland coast north of the Tropic of Capricorn (central Queensland).

NOTES:
Skinny queenfish yield surprisingly little flesh, even in large fish.

Minimum Size: 30cm.   **Bag Limit: 10.**

Rosy jobfish
(King snapper)

Marketing name: King snapper

Pristipomoides filamentosus

DESCRIPTION:
Rosy jobfish grow to more than 100cm (6.5kg). They are
rosy pink over the back, fading to a pinkish-white belly. The
scales are marked to give a speckled appearance. Dorsal
and pectoral fins are flushed with yellow.

HABITAT:
Rosy jobfish are found in coastal waters along the
Queensland east coast.

**The most popular saltwater fishing locations in
Queensland are Moreton Bay (21.7%),
Sunshine Coast (20.3%), Gold Coast (18.4%),
Wide Bay-Burnett (17.1%) and Far North (9.4%).**
— Source: QFMA Recreational Fishing Survey 1997

Minimum Size: 40cm.

Bag Limit: Nil.

Blue threadfin
(Cooktown salmon)

Marketing name: Blue threadfin

Eleutheronema tetradactylum

DESCRIPTION:
Blue threadfin grow to 120cm (18.5kg). Colouration is silvery-blue along the back graduating to silvery-white on the belly. Pectoral fins are yellow with three to four thread-like filaments located below. Separate dorsal fins and the tail are rimmed with blue-black. Blue threadfin are distinct from king threadfin in having fewer and shorter filaments.

HABITAT:
Blue threadfin are found along the Queensland coast from Noosa in the south to the Gulf of Carpentaria. They readily enter tidal rivers and estuaries.

NOTES:
Blue threadfin, like king threadfin, form the basis of an important commercial fishery, and are important recreational fish.

DPI FISHERIES

Minimum Size: 40cm.   **Bag Limit: Nil.**

King threadfin
(Burnett River salmon, Blind salmon)

Marketing name: King threadfin

Polydactylus sheridani

DESCRIPTION:
King threadfin grow to more than 185cm (30kg). They are grey-blue along their backs, becoming silvery below. The lateral line in king threadfin is very distinct. Two, separate, dorsal fins are each set on a hump along the back. Pectoral fins are orange with five, long, highly specialised filaments at the base of each fin. King threadfin are distinct from the similar blue threadfin in having these five long filaments (blue threadfin have three to four shorter filaments).

HABITAT:
Ranging from Noosa in the south, along the Queensland coast to Torres Strait and into the Gulf of Carpentaria, king threadfin prefer the lower reaches of tidal rivers and mangrove flats in tropical waters.

NOTES:
The highly specialised, thread-like filaments are used to locate food along the bottom.

FISH GUIDE   109

DPI FISHERIES

Minimum Size: Nil.　　　　　　　　　　　　　　**Bag Limit: Nil.**

Gummy shark
(Smooth dog shark, Sweet William)

Marketing name: Gummy shark (flake)

Mustelus antarcticus

DESCRIPTION:

Gummy sharks are small, slender sharks, growing to about 175cm (25kg). Colouration is grey above, usually with small white spots, shading to white on the belly. The gummy shark's main food sources are worms and small crustaceans, and, as a result, its teeth are blunt and flattened, forming pavement-like crushing plates common to fish with similar diets.

HABITAT:

Gummy sharks usually inhabit deep, offshore waters, but may also be found in shallow, coastal areas. Although a more southerly species, gummy sharks are found as far north as the Swains Reefs.

NOTES:

Gummy sharks are more important as a commercial species, often marketed as "flake" or boneless fish fillets.

Minimum Size: 30cm.   **Bag Limit: 30.**

Snapper
(Cockney, Red bream, Squire, Schnapper, Nobby)

Marketing name: Snapper

Pagrus auratus

DESCRIPTION:

Snapper grow to more than 130cm (19.5kg). Young fish are commonly called squire (*photo next page*) and are distinct from larger adult fish in having bright blue spots scattered over the upper sides of their bodies, and the lack of a hump over the nape. The blue spots gradually disappear as fish grow, the snout becomes bulbous and a hump forms over the nape. Otherwise, colouration varies from rosy pink to red-brown with pink-flushed fins.

HABITAT:

Snapper are more southerly fish, ranging in Queensland from the Capricorn-Bunker reef groups to the New South Wales border. Both snapper and squire prefer inshore and offshore rocky reefs. Squire also occupy sheltered waters in bays and harbours, moving seaward as they mature.

NOTES:

Although generally referred to as different fish, squire and snapper are the same species, squire being young snapper.

Minimum Size: 30cm. **Bag Limit: 30.**

Snapper
(Squire)
Marketing name: Snapper

DESCRIPTION: Squire are juvenile snapper. They are not a species in their own right. See previous page for details.

DPI FISHERIES

Minimum Size: Nil.　　　　　　　　　**Bag Limit: Nil.**

Sole

Marketing name: Sole (various)

Various

DESCRIPTION:

Sole belong to a group of fishes called flatfishes. As their name suggests, they have flattened bodies and are bottom-dwelling. All Queensland soles are right-eyed, having both eyes on the right side of the body. Sole range from 30cm to 50cm, depending on the species. All species are suitably coloured and patterned to conceal them in their selected habitat (the sea bottom).

HABITAT:

Most sole are widely distributed along the Queensland coastline.

NOTES:

Sole are almost exclusively caught as byproduct from the trawl industry.

DPI FISHERIES

Minimum Size: 30cm.   **Bag Limit: Nil.**

Grass sweetlip
(Snapper bream, Brown sweetlip, Grey sweetlip)

Marketing name: Emperor

Lethrinus fletus

DESCRIPTION:
Grass sweetlip grow to 70cm (5.6kg) and are browny-grey with darker brown blotches and streaks along their sides. Upon death, grass sweetlip fade to a plain grey colour. Each scale carries a brown spot, giving the fish a reticulated pattern. The cheeks are covered in small white dots. Fine blue lines radiate from the eyes (typical of this species). Some of these blue lines may cross the snout.

HABITAT:
Adult grass sweetlip are found in reef waters all along the Queensland coast, although they are more abundant in southern and central Queensland.

NOTES:
Younger fish (up to 20cm) inhabit inshore seagrass beds of eelgrass (*Zostera* sp.).

DPI FISHERIES

Minimum Size: 30cm.　　　　　　　　**Bag Limit: Nil.**

Tailor
(Bluefish)

Marketing name: Tailor

Pomatomus saltatrix

DESCRIPTION:
Tailor grow to 120cm (over 12kg), although they are more commonly caught much smaller. Colouration is pale silvery green along the back graduating to a silvery belly. Tailor have large, powerful jaws equipped with sharp canine teeth.

HABITAT:
Tailor are found in the southern part of Queensland, from Fraser Island south, where they form the basis of a commercial and recreational fishery. Juveniles, called "choppers", enter bays and estuaries.

NOTES:
Tailor are voracious predators and are known to partake in feeding frenzies along coastal beaches when food fish are present.

About a fifth of all anglers in Queensland (21.9%) fish at least once a month.
— Source: QFMA Recreational Fishing Survey 1997

DPI FISHERIES

Minimum Size: 23cm.   **Bag Limit: Nil.**

Tarwhine
(Silver bream, Tarwhine bream)

Marketing name: Tarwhine

Rhabdosargus sarba

DESCRIPTION:

Tarwhine grow to 2kg, but are more commonly caught at 1.4kg. Although often mistaken as yellowfin bream, tarwhine are different in having a rounded head profile, yellow speckled horizontal lines along their bodies, and anal fins with 11 or 12 fin rays (instead of the nine or fewer fin rays in yellowfin bream). Body colouration is bright silver with pectoral, pelvic and anal fins being yellow.

HABITAT:

Tarwhine are found along the Queensland east coast south to the New South Wales border. They are found in the surf zone, in bays and estuaries, and on reefs.

Minimum Size: 45cm.

Bag Limit: 10.

Teraglin
(Teraglin Jew, Trag)

Marketing name: Teraglin

Atractoscion aequidens

DESCRIPTION:

Teraglin grow to 19.5kg, but are more commonly caught at 11kg. They are a long, slender fish with yellowish tail, dorsal and anal fins. Colouration is blue-purple along the back and upper sides, graduating to silvery sides and belly. A pink opalescent sheen covers the body.

HABITAT:

Teraglin are strictly off-shore fish. In Queensland, their range extends from Double Island Point to the New South Wales border.

NOTES:

Teraglin are targeted by the more dedicated anglers.

Minimum Size: Nil. **Bag Limit: Nil.**

Long-nosed trevally
(Grunting trevally)

Marketing name: Trevally

Carangoides chrysophrys

DESCRIPTION:
Long-nosed trevally grow to about 50cm. Colouration is olive-green along the back, fading to silvery on the belly. A black spot is present at the top of the gill cover and the anal fin is lined with white on the outer edge, with small white dots along the inner edge. In adults, olive-green dots are often scattered on the lower sides under the pectoral fins.

HABITAT:
Long-nosed trevally are found along the Queensland coast from Cape Moreton north, in estuaries and reef waters.

NOTES:
Long-nosed trevally may "grunt" when handled (as do some of the other trevally species).

Minimum Size: Nil. **Bag Limit: Nil.**

Golden trevally

Marketing name: Golden trevally

Gnathanodon speciosus

DESCRIPTION:
Golden trevally grow to 37kg. They are silvery fish with yellow flushed over their lower flanks. Juveniles are bright yellow with distinct vertical black bars. These bars fade and disappear with age. Adult golden trevally lack the distinctive colouration of the juveniles, but may have a few black spots randomly distributed over their bodies.

HABITAT:
Golden trevally are distributed along the entire Queensland coast, inhabiting estuaries, ocean beaches, rocky and coralline reefs, to outer reef faces.

NOTES:
Golden trevally differ from other trevally in their complete lack of teeth.

DPI FISHERIES

Minimum Size: 38cm. **Bag Limit: 10.**

Bar-cheeked coral trout
(Island trout)

Marketing name: Coral trout

Plectropomus maculatus

DESCRIPTION:
Bar-cheeked coral trout grow to at least 10kg, but are more commonly caught at around 3.4kg. Colouration is reddish-brown to tan or brown bodies, with a profusion of blue dots over the body and fins. These dots become more elongated and darken to brown-black toward the head. Over the cheek there are distinct bars — hence the name bar-cheeked coral trout.

HABITAT:
Bar-cheeked coral trout are found all through the Great Barrier Reef, preferring the coral reef waters, but is more abundant in north Queensland.

NOTES:
As with all coral trout, the bar-cheeked coral trout is a highly prized eating fish.

P. LAYTON

Minimum Size: 38cm.   **Bag Limit: 10.**

Coral trout

Marketing name: Coral trout

Plectropomus leopardus

DESCRIPTION:
Coral trout grow to about 28kg. Colouration varies from black, through to brown-green, tan, orange, pink and red. A profusion of small blue dots, covering their entire upper bodies, is always present. The red or orange colour variation is perhaps the most recognisable form of this species.

HABITAT:
Preferring reef habitats, coral trout are found along the entire Queensland coast.

The Queensland Fisheries Management Authority can be contacted on —
Telephone: 07 3225 1848
Fax: 07 3227 8788
Email: fisheries@qfma.qld.gov.au
Internet: http://www.qfma.qld.gov.au/qfma

DPI FISHERIES

Minimum Size: Nil.   **Bag Limit: Nil.**

Coronation trout
(Lunar-tailed cod, Fairy cod)

Marketing name: Coral trout

Variola louti

DESCRIPTION:

Coronation trout grow to 6.8kg and are brilliantly beautiful fish. Freshly caught fish are spectacularly coloured with bright spots (which may be vermillion to purple in colour), yellow throat and yellow margins on the fins. Body colouration varies from bright red through to orange. A crescent-shaped, brightly yellow-rimmed tail gives it the name of lunar-tailed cod. This feature is more obvious in smaller specimens (about 2.7kg).

HABITAT:

Coronation trout are found throughout Queensland waters, where they inhabit rocky seabeds and coral reefs.

NOTES:

Coronation trout comonly have small clusters of dark cysts in the gut cavity (common to most coral trout). These lumps are tapeworm cysts and do not affect the edibility of the fish. The cysts are destroyed in the cooking process.

Minimum Size: Nil.

Bag Limit: Nil.

Yellowfin tuna
(Allison tuna)

Marketing name: Yellowfin tuna

Thunnus albacares

DESCRIPTION:

Yellowfin tuna grow to at least 200cm (176kg). They are a powerful and streamlined fish, built for speed in open water. Colouration is shimmering blue-black along the back, graduating to silver on the belly. The dorsal and anal fins and finlets (running along the top and bottom of the back of the fish) are bright yellow. With age, the soft (second) dorsal and anal fins elongate to form sickles.

HABITAT:

In Queensland, yellowfin tuna are found all along the coast, out to the Great Barrier Reef.

NOTES:

Yellowfin tuna form the basis of a major commercial fishery in New South Wales. In Queensland, an increasingly popular sport fishery is developing east of Cape Moreton in the south of the State.

DPI FISHERIES

Minimum Size: Nil. **Bag Limit: Nil.**

Turrum

Carangoides fulvoguttatus

DESCRIPTION:
Turrum grow to 126cm (12kg). Adult fish are blue-green along the back, graduating to irridescent green, blue and pink on the lower sides and the belly. Small brassy-coloured spots are scattered over the upper half of the body, and faint vertical bars may be seen (although these bars fade with age). The vertical bars are more obvious in juvenile fish.

HABITAT:
Turrum prefer more tropical waters and are distributed along the Queensland coast from Fraser Island north. They occur over coralline and rocky reefs to depths of 100 metres.

NOTES:
Turrum are sometimes mistaken for giant trevally. They differ in lacking a small patch of tiny scales on the breast.

DPI FISHERIES

Minimum Size: 30cm.   **Bag Limit: 10.**

Black-spot tuskfish
(Blue parrot)

Marketing name: Tuskfish

Choerodon schoenleinii

DESCRIPTION:

Blackspot tuskfish grow to about 90cm (15.9kg). Adult fish differ from juvenile fish in their body colouration, but both are readily identified by a conspicuous black spot located at the base of the soft dorsal fin. Adult fish are blue-green along the back with short blue bars on each scale. The tail is darker blue-purple and the trailing edge of the dorsal fin is golden orange. Juveniles, by contrast, are olive green along the back with yellow bellies. The short blue bars are present on the scales and a series of blue lines can be seen near the eye and mouth.

HABITAT:

Blackspot tuskfish live on coral reefs and over reef flats along the entire Queensland coast.

NOTES:

Blackspot tuskfish are line-fished using crab baits. They are different to parrot fish in having tusk-like teeth, whereas parrot fish have teeth fused into parrot-like beaks.

DPI FISHERIES

Minimum Size: Nil.   **Bag Limit: Nil.**

Blue tuskfish
(Blue-bone)

Choerodon albigena

DESCRIPTION:
Blue tuskfish grow to 71cm (8.2kg) although they are more commonly seen at around 1.8kg. Colouration is olive-green with a creamy-green belly. A paler blotch is located along their backs below the soft dorsal fin, and their "chins" are creamy white. Distinctive blue patches are found on the upper and lower tips of the tail fin and along the top of the dorsal fins.

HABITAT:
Blue tuskfish are found in reef habitats throughout Queensland and the Great Barrier Reef.

NOTES:
Blue tuskfish have bright blue-green bones and teeth.

Minimum Size: 30cm.   **Bag Limit: 10.**

Purple tuskfish
(Grass parrot, Purple parrot)

Marketing name: Tuskfish

Choerodon cephalotes

DESCRIPTION:
Purple tuskfish grow to 38cm. Colouration is quite distinctive. Body colouration is olive green (darker on the head). The face of these fish, on the nose and between the eyes, is crossed with bright blue bars. An orange-red patch is located at the nape, above the pectoral fins, and the back half of the upper body is covered with a smokey-grey "saddle". Blue bars are located on each scale, similar to the blackspot tuskfish.

HABITAT:
Preferring sandy patches and gutters near seagrass beds, purple tuskfish are found along the entire Queensland coast.

NOTES:
Purple tuskfish are commonly line-fished in south-east Queensland, and are excellent eating.

DPI FISHERIES

Minimum Size: 30cm.   **Bag Limit: 10.**

Venus tuskfish
(Parrot fish, Reef parrot, Cockies)

Marketing name: Tuskfish

Choerodon venustus

DESCRIPTION:
Venus tuskfish grow to about 65cm (4.8kg). Body colouration varies but is commonly reddish-brown along the back and over the face, and pink to orange-pink along the sides. Bright blue bars are usually present, encircling the brightly coloured eye and along the lips. White dots uniformly cover the body and, if the fish is frightened or excited, a black smudge may be seen along the gill cover and on the back (below the start of the dorsal fin).

HABITAT:
In Queensland, the range of the venus tuskfish extends from the New South Wales border to Princess Charlotte Bay in the north. They prefer reef environments.

NOTES:
Venus tuskfish are targeted by both commercial and recreational line-fishers.

Minimum Size: Nil.   **Bag Limit: Nil.**

Blue-faced whiptail

(Rainbow, Paradise butterfish, Butterfly bream, False whiptail)

Pentapodus paradiseus

DESCRIPTION:
Blue-faced whiptail grow to about 25cm. They are olive-green-grey along their backs and creamy below, the two colours distinctly separate. A bright yellow band bisects the darker back, running from behind the eye to the tail, where it joins a blue vee-shaped line at the tail base. A small black dot is located at the junction of the vee. The nose is crossed by alternating blue and olive-green bars, and a thin blue line runs along the base of the dorsal fin.

HABITAT:
Blue-faced whiptails are found in near-coastal waters throughout Queensland.

NOTES:
This small fish is commonly caught to be used as bait for larger fish.

DPI FISHERIES

Minimum Size: 23cm.

Bag Limit: Nil.

Golden-lined whiting
(Rough-scaled whiting)

Sillago analis

DESCRIPTION:

Golden-lined whiting grow to 45cm, but are rarely caught at more than 30cm. Very similar to the sand whiting, golden-lined whiting may de distinguished by a wide golden band present below the lateral line. This band fades with death. Present also are small dark saddles over the rear half of the back, although these are not obvious in dead fish. The black spot found at the base of the pectoral fin of sand whiting is absent in golden-lined whiting.

HABITAT:

Golden-lined whiting are found in bays and estuaries from Moreton Bay north.

NOTES:

Golden-lined whiting are often found with sand whiting. They have very distinctive scales — rough to the touch.

DPI FISHERIES

Minimum Size: 23cm.   **Bag Limit: Nil.**

Sand whiting
(Summer whiting, Blue-nosed whiting)

Marketing name: Sand whiting

Sillago ciliata

DESCRIPTION:
Growing to 50cm (1.25kg), the sand whiting is the largest of our whiting species. Sand whiting are uniformly silver, with brassy reflections. The soft dorsal fin is covered by rows of small dark dots, and a dark blotch is located at the base of the pectoral fin. Pelvic and anal fins are yellow.

HABITAT:
Sand whiting are found along the Queensland east coast, preferring sandy seabeds in sheltered areas and along ocean beaches.

NOTES:
Sand whiting search for food by burrowing head-first into the sand.

The most popular freshwater fishing locations are the Far North (14.7%), Brisbane (13.4%), Darling Downs (12.5%), Wide Bay-Burnett (9.7%), the south west/ central west/ north west (9.5%) and Esk/Kilcoy/Boonah regions (9.2%).

— Source: QFMA Recreational Fishing Survey 1997

Minimum Size: Nil.   **Bag Limit: Nil.**

Trumpeter whiting
(Winter whiting)

Marketing name: Trumpeter whiting

Sillago maculata sp.

DESCRIPTION:

Trumpeter whiting are separated into two subspecies: the southern trumpeter whiting (*Sillago maculata maculata*); and the northern trumpeter whiting (*Sillago maculata burrus*). The southern form is illustrated. Both subspecies grow to 30cm and are generally more abundant during the winter months. They are distinguished from other whiting species in having dark blotches over a silvery body, with a prominent silver line running from the gill cover to the tail. The northern subspecies is different to the southern variety in having a black patch on the top of the first dorsal fin, and black borders along the top and bottom of the tail fin. Both subspecies have a diffuse black spot at the base of the pectoral fins.

HABITAT:

Southern trumpeter whiting are found in shallow coastal waters on sandy bottoms and seagrass beds, from the New South Wales border to Cairns in the north. Northern trumpeter whiting are found in similar environments from Cairns north.

NOTES:

Fishing for trumpeter whiting is a particularly popular pastime in southern Queensland.

INDEX

Amberjack 49

Archerfish 16

Australian bass 17

Bar-faced weever 50

Barramundi 18, 51

Bream
    Brown fatlip 95
    Yellow-finned 53

Bug, Moreton Bay 44

Bullrout 20

Carp
    Crucian 35
    European 37
    Koi 36

Catfish
    Eel-tailed 21
    Fork-tailed 22

Cockle 41

Cod
    Barramundi 54
    Black-tipped 55
    Coral 56
    Estuary 57
    Flowery 58
    Honeycomb 59
    Long-finned 60
    Maori 61
    Mary River 23
    Murray 24
    Potato 62
    Purple 63
    Sleepy 25
    Tomato 64
    Yellow-spotted 65

Crab
    Blue swimmer 45
    Female 48
    Male 48
    Mud 46
    Spanner 47

Dart
    Snub-nosed 66
    Southern swallowtail 67

Dolphin fish 68

Eel 26

Emperor
    Red 69
    Red-throat 70
    Spangled 71

Flathead
    Bar-tailed 72
    Dusky 73
    Sand 74

Flounder 75

Garfish
    Three-by-two 76
    River 77
    Snubnosed 78

Grunter
    Barred 80
    Spotted 79

Happy moments spinefoot 52

Hussar 81

Kingfish
    Black 82
    Yellowtail 83

Leatherjacket
    Fan-bellied 84
    Yellow-finned 85

Longtom 86

Luderick 87

Lungfish 27

Mackerel
    Grey 88
    School 89
    Shark 90
    Spanish 91

Mangrove Jack 92

Maori Wrasse
    Hump-headed 93
    Violet-lined 94

Morwong 95

Mouth Almighty 28

Mullet
    Freshwater 29
    Sea 96

Mulloway 97

Nannygai
    Large-mouth 98
    Small-mouth 99

Oyster 42

Parrot 100

Perch
    Black-spot 101
    Golden 30
    Moses 102
    Pearl 103
    Silver 31
    Spangled 32
    Stripey 104

Pipis 43

Queenfish
    Giant 105
    Skinny 106

Rosy Job Fish 107

Salmon
    Blue Threadfin 108
    King Threadfin 109

Saratoga
    Northern 33
    Southern 34

Scallop
    Ballot's saucer 39
    Fan 40

Shark, Gummy 110

Snapper 111, 112

Sole 113

Sooty Grunter 19

Squire 111, 112

Sweetlip Grass 114

Tailor 115

Tarwhine 116

Teraglin 117

Tilapia 38

Trevally
    Golden 119
    Long-nosed 118

Trout
    Bar-cheeked Coral 120
    Coral 121
    Coronation 122

Tuna, Yellowfin 123

Turrum 124

Tuskfish
    Black-spot 125
    Blue 126
    Purple 127
    Venus 128

Whiptail 129

Whiting
    Golden-lined 130
    Summer/Sand 131
    Trumpeter 132